# Pricing Segmentation and Analytics

# Pricing Segmentation and Analytics

Tudor Bodea and Mark Ferguson

*Pricing Segmentation and Analytics*

Copyright © Business Expert Press, LLC, 2012.

First published in 2012 by
Business Expert Press, LLC
222 East 46th Street, New York, NY 10017
www.businessexpertpress.com

ISBN-13: 978-1-60649-257-4 (paperback)
ISBN-13: 978-1-60649-258-1 (e-book)

DOI 10.4128/9781606492581

A publication in the Business Expert Press Marketing Strategy collection

Collection ISSN: 2150-9654 (print)
Collection ISSN: 2150-9662 (electronic)

Cover design by Jonathan Pennell
Interior design by Scribe Inc.

First edition: January 2012

10 9 8 7 6 5 4 3 2 1

Printed in the United States of America.

# Abstract

Pricing analytics uses historical sales data with mathematical optimization to set and update prices offered through various channels in order to maximize profit. A familiar example is the passenger airline industry, where a carrier may sell seats on the same flight at many different prices. Pricing analytics practices have transformed the transportation and hospitality industries and are increasingly important in industries as diverse as retail, telecommunications, banking, health care, and manufacturing. The aim of this book is to guide students and professionals on how to identify and exploit pricing opportunities in different business contexts.

The first chapter looks at pricing from an economist's viewpoint, beginning with the basic concept of pricing analytics and what type of data are needed to use this powerful science. Next, the common assumptions regarding the customer population's willingness-to-pay are discussed along with the price-response functions that result from this assumption. From the price-response functions, we show how to estimate price elasticity and how it differs at the product, firm, and industry levels as well as in the short term versus long term. Basic price optimization techniques are then explored.

The second chapter looks at these same topics but from a more practical standpoint, with examples provided from several industries and organizations.

The third chapter is on dynamic pricing, with a special emphasis on the most common application: markdown pricing. Similar to the first two chapters, both the theory and the application aspects will be covered.

The fourth chapter covers the new field of customized pricing analytics, where a firm responds to a request-for-bids or request-for-proposals with a customized price response. In this situation, the firm only has historical win/loss data, and traditional methods involving price elasticity do not apply. The pricing analytics methodology is described in a step-by-step process from an actual application.

The final chapter covers the relevant aspects of behavioral science to pricing. Examples include the asymmetry of joy/pain that customers feel in response to price decreases/increases. A set of best pricing practices are provided based on these behavioral responses. Finally, the appendices contain more details on the commonly used tool of logistic regression and the open source statistical software environment R.

# Keywords

Segmentation, revenue management, price optimization, price elasticity, promotions, pricing

# Contents

*I would like to thank my coauthors, colleagues, and students who have helped me learn and explore this exciting topic. Special thanks goes to my wife Kathy, and daughters Grace and Tate, for their love, encouragement, and support.*

—Mark Ferguson

*I would like to thank my coauthors and former colleagues at InterContinental Hotels Group and Predictix for offering me the opportunity to work with them. I would also like to acknowledge the debt I owe to my family—I have become who I am because of them.*

—Tudor Bodea

*To all those who inspired and believed in us—*
*we are grateful for all your support.*

# CHAPTER 1

# Theory of Pricing Analytics

How do managers in a firm decide on the prices to charge for the products or services they sell? For some firms, the pricing decision is made at the top level of the management team with little flexibility for the sales force, marketing team, or supply chain partners (distributors or retailers) to make adjustments. Apple's fixed pricing for its popular iPhone and iPad products is a good example of this practice. For other firms, it may appear to the customer that pricing is left entirely up to the individual sales person. This happens frequently in the business-to-business (B2B) market, such as the pricing for a major software implementation by a software vendor or consulting company. The price quoted for a new car from a dealership is an example from the business-to-consumer (B2C) market. Even in these situations, however, there is almost always some price guidance provided by a division level or corporate pricing team. Thus most large firms have some department or team whose primary responsibility is to determine the price, or price range, to charge for the firm's products. The group may reside under many different branches of the corporate organizational structure, such as marketing, operations, or finance, and its members may or may not have pricing in their job titles. It is also common for this group of professionals to have access to some historical pricing and sales data, even if this information is not currently being used in the price setting process.

Pricing analytics involves the use of historical data to determine the best prices to set for future sales. In this chapter, our focus is on the theory behind pricing analytics. In the next chapter, we discuss how the practice of pricing analytics may sometimes differ from the theory. Our focus in both of these chapters is on the setting of a base price for a single product. An example would be the regular price to charge for a nonperishable product

For consistency and where appropriate, we use the same notation in this chapter as Phillips (2005a).

sold through a retail store. We cover more specific applications of pricing analytics such as dynamic pricing, markdown pricing, and customized B2B pricing in later chapters. We also save our discussion of the important topic of behavioral responses to pricing for a later chapter. While it is often difficult to apply the techniques described in this chapter directly, a good understanding of the theory behind pricing analytics is crucial to successful applications of the techniques described later in the book.

## The Microeconomists' View of Consumer-Purchasing Decisions

What makes a consumer decide to purchase a product or to choose one product over all the other alternatives? Economists use the term *consumer utility* to represent the value that a particular product or service provides to a customer. Utility is often represented in monetary values. For example, at a particular point in time, a consumer may derive a utility of $1 for a can of Coca-Cola and a utility of $0.90 from a can of Pepsi.

### Willingness-to-Pay

Another term that is commonly used in the pricing field is the consumer's maximum *willingness-to-pay* (WTP), or the maximum price at which the consumer would buy a good. Often, consumer utility and willingness-to-pay are terms that are used interchangeably. Thus if the consumer is at a store that only sells cans of Coca-Cola, microeconomic theory says that the consumer will purchase a can if the price is less than or equal to $1 (we are assuming away budget constraints in this example, i.e., the consumer is not prohibited from purchasing the product because of budgetary constraints). If the store sells cans of both Coca-Cola and Pepsi, then the consumer will purchase the brand that maximizes her remaining utility after subtracting the purchase price. For example, if a can of Coca-Cola is priced at $0.75 but a can of Pepsi is $0.50, then the customer purchases the can of Pepsi because ($0.90 − $0.50) > ($1.00 − $0.75).

### Consumer Search Cost

In addition to a side-by-side comparison of the prices of different brands of a particular product, consumers are often aware that alternative brands or prices are available at other locations or through other channels. In the previous example, we assumed that the consumer will purchase one of the brands of soda from the store she is currently in. Suppose, however, that the consumer knows that the store across the street sells cans of Pepsi for $0.40. Will the consumer delay the purchase of a can of soda and cross the street to save an extra $0.10? To answer this question, economists have defined a "search cost" to represent the hassle of searching and purchasing the product from another location or source. Thus the consumer will still purchase the can of Pepsi from the store as long as ($0.90 – $0.50) > ($0.90 – $0.40 – search cost).

What makes pricing challenging is that a particular customer's utility for products may change over time depending on factors such as the season, the weather, the overall economic climate, or the current competitive environment in our industry. In addition, different consumers typically have different WTPs and different search costs (termed *heterogeneous customers* in the economics literature), and we seldom have the capability to set a personalized price for each specific consumer. Even if we did have the capability to set customized prices for each specific consumer, they do not make it a practice to tell us what their utilities are for our products. This is rational; consumers recognize that firms that know their maximum WTP for a product can set a specific price for each consumer equal to that consumer's maximum WTP. Thus the practice of pricing analytics has evolved to improve upon historical pricing performance while taking into account the realities mentioned earlier.

## The Pricing Analytics Process

Pricing analytics is an iterative process using historical price/demand data to adjust the price of a product in order to maximize profits by analyzing the trade-off among price, volume, and cost. In general, the field has moved toward the term *price analytics* and away from the term *price optimization* because optimization implies that it is possible to analytically determine the single price that will maximize profits with a reasonable degree of confidence. In practice, there is always uncertainty about whether a given price is the "right" price. Still, approximating the optimal price is the goal. Determining the profit-maximizing price requires a combination of analytical rigor and managerial judgment to understand the trade-offs among prices, costs, and customer response. An overview of this process is shown in Figure 1.1.

The approach behind pricing analytics is to formulate pricing problems as constrained optimization problems that can be solved by standard techniques. The following elements are required:

- A price-response function that describes how customers are expected to respond to our pricing actions
- An objective function that specifies what we are trying to achieve (maximize profits, meet a market share target, etc.)
- A set of constraints that limit what we can do (capacity, capital, margin, etc.)

The goal of pricing analytics is to provide the right price for every product, for every customer segment, through every channel. For example, it may be better to set a different price for a large-revenue customer in the Northwest who orders from the firm directly than for a smaller customer in the Northeast who orders through a distributor. Some banks will even quote different interest rates to the same customer if she arrives via an online search versus in person at the local branch office. The first step before determining a profit-maximizing price, however, is to determine how customers will react to a price change. This involves the estimation of price-response functions from historical price/demand data.

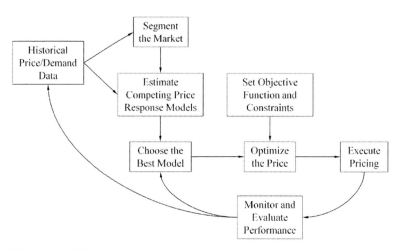

*Figure 1.1.The pricing analytics process.*

### Historical Price/Demand Data

The data typically used in a pricing analytics process is historical transaction data that shows how much demand occurred for a given time period, a given location, and a given price. Care must be taken to ensure the accuracy of this dataset before beginning the pricing analytics process. For example, the dataset should be tested for outliers (data points that appear to be statistical anomalies) and each identified outlier should be investigated to determine if it should remain in the dataset. In addition, there is often an issue with incomplete dataset or missing values. There is a long history of research on how to test for outliers and how to handle missing values in statistical estimation projects. Finally, the price/demand data that most firms have available is sales data, not demand data. This happens when the product is out of stock and demand for the product during the time it is out of stock is not recorded. In such cases, the demand data must be unconstrained before it can be used to estimate price-response functions. Since data integrity is not a focus of this book, we simply offer a warning to the reader to plan on spending a significant portion of the project duration simply extracting, cleaning, and unconstraining the datasets. Additional types of data used for pricing analytics are detailed in Table 2.1.

### Estimating and Choosing the Best Price-Response Models

After the historical price/demand data has been extracted and evaluated as a good representation of past consumer demand, it can be used to estimate alternative price-response functions. The reason for estimating alternative functions is because we do not know, a priori, which price-response function provides the best representation of consumer demand. The estimation and evaluation of price-response functions is a major component of this book.

### Set Objective Function and Constraints and Optimize the Price

Once a price-response function has been estimated and an objective function and constraints are set, the optimization of the price for each specific market segment is typically straightforward. An optimal price is defined as the price (or set of prices) that results in the best value of the objective function while the required resources needed to achieve the objective function value remain within the limits specified by the model constraints. A common example of an objective function with constraints is when a firm seeks to find the price that maximizes profits (objective function) given a specific amount of inventory available (constraint).

### Execute Pricing

While it may appear that price execution is a trivial piece of the pricing analytics process, it is often the step where pricing projects break down in practice. A firm may perform exceptionally well on each of the other steps in the process, but if the right prices are not presented to the right set of consumers in the right way, then the entire pricing analytics process will fail to deliver its projected value. While price execution is not a focus of this book, its importance cannot be overestimated.

### Monitor and Evaluate Performance

As the figure shows, market feedback occurs at two levels. The most immediate feedback is the analysis of alternatives. Here, the effects of the most recent actions should be monitored so that immediate action can be taken if necessary. The second level of feedback updates the parameters of the price-response functions. If the sales of some products are slower than expected, it may indicate that the market is more price responsive than expected and the future market-response curve for that product should be adjusted accordingly.

Now that we have briefly explained each of the steps in the pricing analytics process, we next take a deeper look at the price-response functions that serve as the backbone of the price optimization endeavor.

## The Price-Response Function

As previously discussed, the first step in the pricing analytics process is to collect the historical price/demand data for the product of interest. Using this historical data, the price-response function can be estimated using econometric techniques such as linear or nonlinear regression. The price-response function specifies demand for the product of a single seller as a function of the price offered by that seller (Figure 1.2). This contrasts with the concept of a market demand curve, which specifies how an entire market will respond to changing prices. The distinction is critical because different firms competing in the same market face different price-response functions that are the result of many factors, such as the effectiveness of their marketing campaigns, customer-perceived differences in quality, product differences, and location. Hence, the price-response function may be different even for the same product if the product is sold through different channels or outlets.

In a perfectly competitive market, the price response faced by an individual seller is a vertical line at the market price. If the seller prices above the market price, her demand drops to zero. If the seller prices below the market price, her demand is equal to the entire market. In a perfectly competitive market, the seller has no pricing decision—the price is set by the operation of the larger market.

The price-response functions that most companies face are not necessarily linear over the entire price range as shown in Figure 1.2, but they do demonstrate some degree of smooth price response over the entire range of possible prices. As price increases, demand declines until it reaches zero at some satiating price. As price decreases, the demand approaches the maximum market size for that product and location.

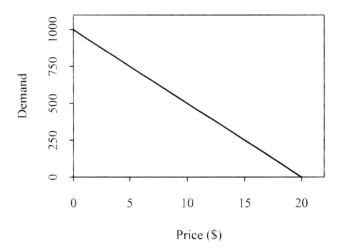

*Figure 1.2. Linear price-response function.*

### Choosing the Best Price-Response Function

When choosing a price-response function to fit to the historical price/demand data, you are implicitly making assumptions about customer behavior. It is worthwhile to understand these assumptions so that we can judge which candidate price-response function is appropriate for the application. The most important of these assumptions involves the distribution of the consumers' WTP. For pricing analytics, we assume that consumers' WTP has a known distribution, $w(p)$, across the entire population of consumers. Exactly how consumers' WTP is distributed across the potential customer population is an important decision in the pricing analytics process. Figure 1.3 shows a distribution of WTP where consumers are evenly distributed across the entire range of possible prices. Here, $P$ is the maximum price consumers are willing to pay for the product/service they are requesting.

Note that $0 \leq w(p) \leq 1$ for all nonnegative values of $p$. Let $D = d(0)$ be the maximum demand achievable. In concrete terms, $D$ is the sales expected to materialize at a price of zero and reflects the market size. We can derive the price-response function, $d(p)$, from the WTP distribution via

$d(k)$ = the demand expected to materialize at a price $p = k$

= the number of people who have WTP greater than price $p = k$

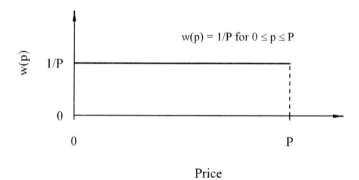

Figure 1.3. Uniform WTP distribution.

$= D \cdot$ the area of the WTP distribution to the right of price $p = k$

$$= D \cdot \int_{k}^{P} w(p)dp.$$

For the uniform WTP distribution shown in Figure 1.3, the fraction of the population with WTP $\geq p$ is $(P - p)/P$, or, $1 - p/P$ (see Figure 1.4). Thus the total population with WTP $\geq p$ is $d(p) = D - D \cdot p/P$.

It is important to understand what an assumption about the underlying consumer WTP distribution implies. For the uniform WTP distribution depicted in Figure 1.3 and Figure 1.4, this choice of distribution requires that an equal percentage of the total consumer population is willing to purchase a product at every possible price point. If we used this distribution for our Coca-Cola example, and the maximum that anyone is willing to pay for a can of Coke is $5, then a uniform distribution implies that there are just as many consumers who are willing to pay but will pay no more than $5 for a can of Coke as there are consumers who will pay but will pay no more than $1. This is probably not the case for the general population. Most of us would fall in some middle range of WTP rather than be evenly distributed over a broad range of possible prices. Thus perhaps a more plausible WTP distribution assumption is one that groups the largest percentage of the consumers around some mean value, placing very small probabilities at the low- and high-end extremes. Such a distribution is often called a bell-curve distribution as

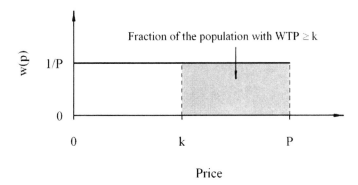

*Figure 1.4. Density of demand at price k from a uniform WTP distribution.*

shown in Figure 1.5. The reason it is called a bell-curve distribution is because the graph of its probability density function looks like a bell. The normal distribution is the most common of the bell-shaped distributions. If $P$ and $k$ were $20 and $10, respectively, one could interpret the WTP distribution shown in Figure 1.5 as saying that there are few consumers with a maximum WTP of $15 or more for the product represented. On the other hand, there is a large percentage of the consumer population with a maximum WTP between $5 and $15.

Now that we have explored a few WTP distribution assumptions, we can explain how the choice of a WTP distribution results in different price-response functions.

### Common Price-Response Functions

Choosing and estimating the right price-response function is arguably the most difficult part of any pricing analytics project. In this chapter, we present four commonly used functions. We save for the next chapter a discussion of exactly how to estimate the functions and how to choose the best function.

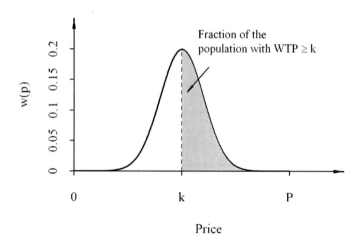

*Figure 1.5. Density of demand at price k from a normal WTP distribution.*

## Linear Price-Response Function

The linear price-response function shown in Figure 1.6 can be represented by the same familiar equation used for linear regression:

$$d(p) = D + m \cdot p, \tag{1.1}$$

where $D$ represents the intercept term, $p$ is the independent variable, and $m = -D/P$ is the slope for $0 < p < P$. It is commonly used in practice mainly because it is easy to estimate by applying simple linear regression on the historical price/demand data.

## Constant-Elasticity Price-Response Function

A second commonly used price-response function is the constant-elasticity function, which has a point elasticity (defined in the next section) that is the same at all prices. It is based on exponential WTP distribution. The price-response function is

$$d(p) = C \cdot p^{\varepsilon}, \tag{1.2}$$

where $C > 0$ and $\varepsilon$ are parameter values that are estimated by fitting equation (1.2) to the price/demand data. Some sample constant-elasticity price-response functions are shown in Figure 1.7.

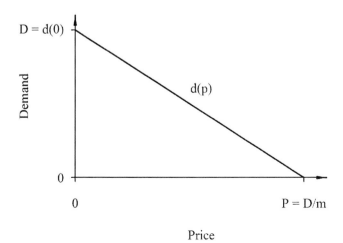

*Figure 1.6. Linear price-response function.*

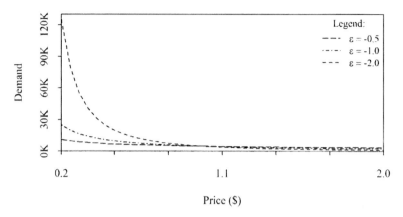

*Figure 1.7. Constant-elasticity price-response functions (C = 5,000).*

Both linear and constant-elasticity price-response functions are useful for *local* demand estimation but are often not realistic *global* price-response models. When global demand estimation over the entire range of prices is needed, we need a function that is based on the bell-curve WTP distribution shown in Figure 1.5. The price-response function that results from a bell-curve WTP distribution has a reverse S shape, as shown in Figure 1.8.

For price-response curves with a reverse S shape, there are diminishing returns when making large price decreases, as can be seen by the flatness of the curve in Figure 1.8 for prices on the left side of the graph. Similarly, the curve is flat for relatively high prices. Changes in price in the middle range, however, often results in significant changes in demand. One way to think about this is to imagine the population of Coca-Cola and Pepsi drinkers. There is a small segment of very loyal Pepsi or Coca-Cola drinkers that will not consider the other brand for any difference in price (the extreme left or right parts of the curve), while there is a larger segment of consumers that will change their purchase decision between the two if the price difference is large enough (the middle section of the curve). We will cover two of these reverse S-shaped functions here, the power and the logit functions.

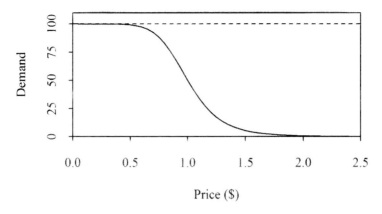

*Figure 1.8. Reverse S-shaped price-response function.*

Power Price-Response Function

The power price-response function is one function with the reverse S shape:

$$d(p) = \alpha \cdot D/(p^\beta + \alpha), \qquad (1.3)$$

where $D > 0$, $\alpha$, and $\beta$ are parameter values estimated by fitting equation (1.3) to the price/demand data. The power price-response function is shown for different values of $\beta$ in Figure 1.9. Higher values of $\beta$ represent more price-sensitive markets. As $\beta$ grows larger, the market approaches

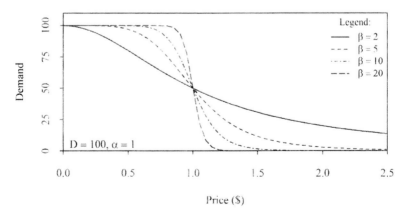

*Figure 1.9. Power price-response functions.*

the perfectly competitive price-response function. Different values of $\alpha$ shift the curves left and right along the horizontal *price*-axis.

Logit Price-Response Function

The second common price-response curve that has a reverse S shape functional form is the logit function:

$$d(p) = \frac{C \cdot e^{a+b \cdot p}}{1 + e^{a+b \cdot p}}, \tag{1.4}$$

where $C > 0$, $a$, and $b$ are parameter values that are estimated by fitting equation (1.4) to the price/demand data. The shape of the logit function is similar to the shape of the power functions shown in Figure 1.9. One advantage the logit function has over the power function is that it can be estimated using logistics regression, a methodology that is commonly available in most statistical software packages. Table 1.1 summarizes the commonly used price-response functions.

The most useful feature of price-response functions is that, once estimated, they can be used to determine the price sensitivity of a product or how demand will change in response to a change in price. In the next section, we look at some ways that price sensitivity is measured.

*Table 1.1. Price-Response Functions*

| Price-response function | Formula | WTP distribution |
|---|---|---|
| Linear | $d(p) = D + m \cdot p$ | Uniform |
| Constant elasticity | $d(p) = C \cdot p^{\varepsilon}$ | Exponential |
| Power | $d(p) = \dfrac{\alpha \cdot D}{p^{\beta} + \alpha}$ | Weibull |
| Logit | $d(p) = \dfrac{C \cdot e^{a+b \cdot p}}{1 + e^{a+b \cdot p}}$ | Gumbel |

## Measures of Price Sensitivity

Once we have some historical price and demand data, the pricing analytics process described in Figure 1.1 shows that the next steps are to segment the market and to estimate the market response. The market response is typically estimated by measuring how a change in the price of a product results in a change in demand. Similarly, segmenting the market refers to finding different consumer attributes where consumers with similar attributes have the same (or similar) price-demand responses.

Estimating the market response and determining if different consumer segments have different responses require some measure of how demand changes with price. The simplest measurement is to simply take the slope of the price-response function at some given price. The slope, defined as the change in the y-axis divided by the change in the x-axis, measures the local rate of change of the price-response function at a particular price (price $p$ in Figure 1.10). The slope of the price-response function is always negative and can be measured for a continuous price-response function by taking its derivative. If we denote the price-response function by $d(p)$, a reasonable local estimator of the change in demand that would result from a small change in price (changing the price from $p1$ to $p2$) is

$$d(p2) - d(p1) \approx d'(p1) \cdot (p2 - p1),$$

$$\text{change in demand} \approx \text{slope} \cdot \text{change in price,}$$

where $d'(p)$ represents the derivative of the price-response function with respect to price. For example, the price-response function in Figure 1.2 can be represented by

$$d(p) = 10,000 - 500 \cdot p.$$

The maximum WTP in this market is $20 and the maximum market size is 10,000. The slope of this function is –500, which can be found by taking the derivative: $d'(p) = -500$. A slope of –500 implies that a $1 increase in the product's price results in a decrease in demand of 500 units. Thus an estimate of how much demand will demand will decrease if we raise the price from $5 to $10 is $|-500 \cdot (\$10 - \$5)|$ or 2,500 units.

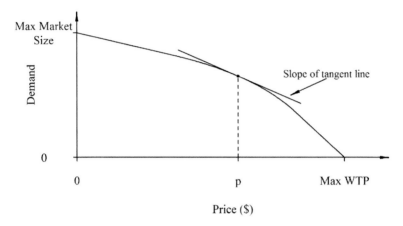

*Figure 1.10. Nonlinear price-response curve.*

While the slope of the price-response function provides a useful measure of price sensitivity, it has a major drawback. The slope of the price-response function depends on the units of measurement being used for both price and demand. Thus slope expressed in gallons/dollar will not be the same as in liters/euro. For this reason, the most common measure of price sensitivity used today is price elasticity. Price elasticity is defined as the ratio of the percentage change in demand to a percentage change in price. Formally, we can write

$$\varepsilon(p1,p2) = (p1 \cdot (d(p2) - d(p1)))/((p2 - p1) \cdot d(p1)). \qquad (1.5)$$

Here, $\varepsilon(p1, p2)$ is called the *arc elasticity* as it requires two prices to calculate. Thus the result will depend on both the old price and the new price. An elasticity of –2 means that a 10% *increase* in price will result in a 20% *decrease* in demand and an elasticity of –0.6 means that a 10% decrease in price will result in a 6% increase in demand. We can also derive a *point elasticity* at price $p$ by taking the limit of equation (1.5) as $p2$ approaches $p1$:

$$\varepsilon(p) = p \cdot d'(p)/d(p). \qquad (1.6)$$

The point elasticity is useful as a local estimate of the change in demand resulting from a small change in price.

### Properties of Elasticity

- Always < 0. The downward-sloping property (the slope of price-response functions is always negative) guarantees that demand always changes in the opposite direction from price. Thus the minus sign on the right-hand side of equation (1.5) guarantees that $\varepsilon(p1,p2) < 0$.
- Independent of units. Elasticity of gasoline will be the same measured in gallons/$ or liters/euro.
- Depends on the price at which it is measured.
- Low elasticity. $|\varepsilon| < 1$ means consumers are price insensitive.
- High elasticity. $|\varepsilon| > 1$ means consumers are price sensitive.
- Depends on time period of measurement. For most products, short-run elasticity is lower than long-run elasticity because buyers have more flexibility to adjust to higher prices in the long run.
- Depends on level of measurement (see Table 1.2).
- Industry elasticity may be low but individual product elasticity is always higher.

Table 1.3 and Figure 1.11 show some elasticities that have been estimated for various goods and services at the industry level. Some products are very inelastic—salt, for example, is a relatively cheap commodity-type product and customers do not change the amount of salt they purchase very much in response to market price changes.

Price elasticities will be different for different market segments. For example, price elasticities are generally higher for the same type of products for coupon users than that for nonusers.

### Table 1.2. Estimated Price Elasticities at the Industry and Brand Level

| Product | Elasticity |
|---|---|
| Soft drinks[1] | –0.80 to –1.00 |
| Coca-Cola[2] | –3.80 |
| Mountain Dew[3] | –4.40 |

*Table 1.3. Estimated Price Elasticities for Various Goods*

| Product | Mean | Median | Number of observations | Length of run |
|---|---|---|---|---|
| Petrol[4] | −0.25 | | 46 | Short run |
| Residential electricity[5] | −0.35 | −0.28 | 123 | Short run |
| Residential water[6] | −0.41 | −0.35 | 314 | |
| | −0.51 | | 124 | |
| Beer[7] | −0.46 | −0.35 | 139 | |
| Cigarettes[8] | −0.48 | | 523 | |
| | | −0.4 | 368 | Short run |
| | | −0.44 | 155 | Long run |
| Petrol[9] | −0.64 | | 51 | Long run |
| Wine[10] | −0.72 | −0.58 | 141 | |
| Spirits[11] | −0.74 | −0.68 | 136 | |
| Residential electricity[12] | | | | |
| | −0.85 | −0.81 | 125 | Long run |
| Branded products[13] | −1.76 | | 337 | |

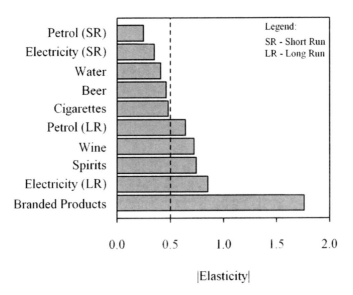

*Figure 1.11. Estimated price elasticities for various goods (absolute values).*

The elasticity of the linear price-response function is $m \cdot p/(D + m \cdot p)$, which ranges from 0 at $p = 0$ and approaches negative infinity as $p$ approaches $P$. The elasticity of the constant-elasticity price-response function is, wait for it, constant for every price within the range of the function. The elasticity of the logit price-response function is $b \cdot p/(1 + e^{a + b \cdot p})$.

### The Impact of Elasticity on Revenue

Knowing the elasticity of a product around a certain price point tells us something about how the revenue from the sales of that product will change with small price changes. In particular, if

- $|\varepsilon| < 1$ (inelastic), raising price will increase revenue;
- $|\varepsilon| = 1$, revenue is independent of price;
- $|\varepsilon| > 1$ (elastic), raising price will decrease revenue.

Now that we have chosen a WTP distribution, estimated the corresponding price-response function, and estimated the price elasticity, it is finally time to return to our original objective—to optimize the price so as to maximize profit.

# Price Optimization

### The Objective Function

Before determining the optimal price, firms must establish their strategic goals, one that specifies what they are trying to accomplish in the market. Examples include maximizing the total profit, maximizing the revenue, meeting some predetermined market share target, or some combination of these three. Normally, we assume that the objective is to maximize total profit:

$$\underset{p}{Max} \; Profit(p) = \underset{p}{Max} \; (p-c) \cdot d(p). \tag{1.7}$$

The total profit as a function of price is hill-shaped, with a single peak, as shown in Figure 1.12. Let $p^*$ represent the price that maximizes the total profit. Not surprisingly, the firm's profit is negative when the price is below its unit cost of $5.

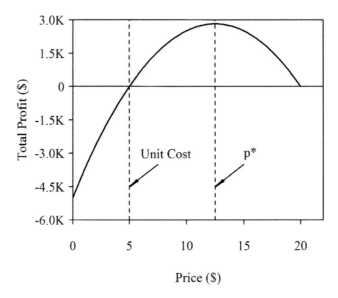

**Figure 1.12. Profits as a function of price.**

### The Price Optimization Problem

A widget-making company sells widgets through a single channel. The unit costs are constant at $5 per widget and the demand is governed by the linear price-response function represented in Figure 1.2:

$$d(p) = 1,000 - 50 \cdot p.$$

The firm's profit as a function of price is

$$\text{Max } \underset{p}{\text{Profit}}(p) = (p-5) \cdot (1,000 - 50 \cdot p)$$

$$= -50 \cdot p^2 + 1,250 \cdot p - 5,000. \tag{1.8}$$

The profit maximizing price is found by taking the derivative of the profit function and setting it to zero. To understand why, refer back to the curve in Figure 1.12. The curve in the graph represents the profit function and the highest point in the curve is where the slope changes from positive to negative. The slope of the curve is found by taking the derivative of it with respect to price, thus we take the derivative of the profit function and set it equal to zero. Applying this technique to equation (1.8) gives

$$-100p + 1250 = 0,$$

$$p^* = \$12.50.$$

Solving equation (1.7), we find $p^*$ such that

$$\text{profit}'(p^*) = d'(p^*)(p^* - c) + d(p^*) = 0.$$

By rearranging the formula, we get the classic economics result:

$$p^*d'(p^*) + d(p^*) = cd'(p^*),$$

marginal revenue = marginal cost.

### Elasticity and Optimization

In the last section, we saw how elasticity can be used to determine if a price change will increase or decrease revenue. Elasticity can also provide guidance on when to lower or raise prices so as to maximize profits. By combining the equation of point elasticity with the condition that the derivative of the profit function should be set equal to zero, we get

$$(p^* - c)/p^* = -1/\varepsilon(p^*). \tag{1.9}$$

The left side of the equation is the margin per unit expressed as a fraction of price, also known as the gross margin ratio. To help illustrate the usefulness of this formulation, consider a seller seeking to maximize her total profit. Under what relative values of her current price, her cost $c$, and her point elasticity $\varepsilon(p)$ should she raise her price to increase her profit? Under what conditions should she lower her price or keep her price the same? The answers are provided by the following set of rules:

$(p - c)/p = -1/\varepsilon(p) \rightarrow p$ is optimal (don't change price).

$(p - c)/p < -1/\varepsilon(p) \rightarrow p$ is too low—profit can be increased by raising price (gain in per-unit margin > loss in sales). This will always be true when $|\varepsilon(p)| < 1$.

$(p - c)/p > -1/\varepsilon(p) \rightarrow p$ is too high—contribution can be increased by lowering price (gain in sales will outweigh loss in per-unit margin).

Note that all rules are local since $\varepsilon(p)$ changes as the price changes.

### Example

- A two-liter bottle of Coca-Cola has a short-run elasticity of –3.8. The optimal price is one that provides a margin of $(1/3.8) = 26\%$.
- The short run elasticity of heroin in Norway has been estimated to be approximately –1.25. The optimal price for dealers should provide a margin of $(1/1.25) = 80\%$.

With equation (1.9), we can get the formula for the optimal price of

$$p* = \frac{\varepsilon(p*)}{1 + \varepsilon(p*)} \cdot c. \qquad (1.10)$$

### Customer Segmentation and Price Optimization

Up to this point, we have assumed that the population of consumers differs in its willingness-to-pay but not in its price sensitivities. This assumption is implied when we use only one price-response function to represent all the consumer population. The real value in price optimization, however, often comes from identifying microsegments of consumers who have different price sensitivities (coupon users versus noncoupon users, for example). To find these microsegments, the historical price demand dataset is divided up into possible different segments based on some customer attributes other than price. For example, a dataset may be divided into two groups based on the attribute that a customer belongs to the firm's loyalty program or not. Once the dataset is divided into different segments, the data from each segment can then be fit to different price-response functions. There are various ways to test whether the resulting fits of the microsegments to different price-response functions are better than the fit of the entire dataset to a single price-response function. If dividing the dataset into the microsegments does result in better fits, then prices can be optimized for each segment using their specific price-response function.

One example of using price segmentation in the price analytics process has been applied at a grocery store chain. Previous studies have shown that consumers who shop at a grocery store after 5 p.m. on weekdays are generally less price sensitive than consumers who shop on weekdays before 5 p.m. This finding is intuitive as the consumers who are shopping after 5 p.m. are generally working professionals who are on their way home from work and do not bother to comparison shop, while consumers who shop before 5 p.m. consist of homemakers and retired individuals who, conceivably, are more price conscious and have more time to comparison shop. To take advantage of this knowledge, there is a grocery store chain in Texas that raises the prices of almost all items after 5 p.m. on weekdays and lowers them again before opening the next morning. In the rest of this book, we will frequently return to how price segmentation plays a critical part in the pricing analytics process.

## Chapter Summary

To summarize this chapter, we began with the ultimate goal: to be able to determine different segments of customers based on their price sensitivities and to optimally set a different price for each segment. To accomplish this objective, pricing analytics theory states that we use historical price/demand data to measure and test the price elasticity of different segments. Price elasticity is the percentage change in demand for a percentage change in price. Thus larger (negative) values of price elasticity represent price-sensitive segments while smaller (negative) values represent price-insensitive segments. Once the price elasticity for each customer segment is known, optimizing the price for each segment is straightforward.

To estimate price elasticities from historical price/demand data, we must make assumptions about how the maximum willingness-to-pay for a product is distributed over the entire set of potential customers. Different assumptions about the willingness-to-pay distribution result in different price-response functions that will be estimated using the price/demand data. Some price-response functions are simpler and easier to estimate than others, but care must be taken that we are accurately modeling true buying behavior. Thus it is common to evaluate several potential price-response functions on the same set of estimation data (a subset, but not all, of the historical price/demand dataset) to determine which function provides the best fit for the remaining holdout sample. Once a price-response function has been selected, price elasticities for each segment can be calculated, statistical significance tests can be performed, and price optimization can be performed for each significant segment.

# CHAPTER 2

# The Practice of Pricing Analytics

In chapter 1 we provided a brief summary of the theory of pricing analytics. While informative, this discussion has not provided you or your organization with advice on important questions such as "Am I ready to start experimenting with pricing analytics? If so, how can I operationalize some of these theoretical concepts?" or "When should I declare myself satisfied with the progress I made?" To help gain an understanding of what these and other similar questions require of an organization, we open this chapter with a few statements on what developing organizational pricing capabilities entails. We then provide a few practical examples of how to estimate the price elasticity of demand. Since, in practice, pricing analytics is typically enacted through price promotions, we also touch on the estimation of the promotion effects. In doing so, we approach the task from a theoretical perspective but execute it from a rather practical angle. Last but not least, we conclude the chapter with a few relevant examples.

Developing and sustaining pricing capabilities is a complex task impacted by factors as diverse as the company market position, the vision of its leaders, and the sophistication of its execution mechanisms as reflected by the quality of its people and systems.[1] In what follows, we look into the issues raised by the process of developing pricing capabilities from a narrow yet practical angle. First, following our belief that people are an organization's most valuable asset, we judge the organization's pricing capabilities by the pricing expertise shown by its staff. Second, as the field of pricing analytics is data driven, we also assess an organization's pricing capabilities by the types of data available at its disposal (for relevant examples, see Table 2.1). Our latter choice is motivated by the fact that the types of data an organization makes use of are often a reflection of the sophistication of the support systems that drive the business.

*Table 2.1. Types of Data Used to Make Pricing Decisions*

| Data | Relevance | Details |
|------|-----------|---------|
| **Basics** | | |
| 1. Price/demand data | B2C | Links prices offered to the market performance of a product. Helps build price-response functions. |
| 2. Bid-price data | B2B | Links prices quoted to the outcome of the bid process. Helps build bid-response functions. |
| 3. Pricing guidance and business rules | B2C, B2B | Specify constrains that apply to pricing decisions. |
| 4. Market segmentation intelligence | B2C, B2B | Supports the customization of the price. |
| **Advanced** | | |
| 1. Product and location hierarchies | B2C | Support tier pricing. |
| 2. Special event data | B2C | Provides the timing of special events (e-mail campaigns, Christmas, etc.) and helps unconstrain the demand. |
| 3. Inventory data | B2C | Helps estimate the inventory effects on sales. |
| 4. Out-of-stock data | B2C | Helps unconstrain the demand. |
| 5. Promotion data | B2C | Provides the timing and type of promotion activities. Helps unconstrain the demand. |
| 6. Competitive data | B2C, B2B | Helps link product performance to own and competitors' prices. |
| 7. Click data | B2C | Helps segment products and customers and supports the customization of the price. |

B2C: business-to-consumer pricing; B2B: business-to-business pricing

Stated otherwise, the quality of the business insights derived from the data available typically correlates well with the support systems in place within an organization. We illustrate our approach in the process road-map shown in Figure 2.1.

In the initial stages of acquiring pricing capabilities, companies typically find themselves at point A in Figure 2.1. Here, they have little or no pricing expertise, since no dedicated personnel exist to strengthen this function. Furthermore, no data are usually available to support the practice of the function. Ironically, in some cases, companies at this stage actually collect and own the market data needed for pricing analytics, but the lack of pricing expertise makes it difficult to transform this latent information into actionable market decisions. In the evolving business environments in which most organizations operate, companies that stay for too long in point A are usually perceived as high-risk companies, since they seem to be unable to fully align with their customers' needs.

Early attempts to adapt to the new business realities usually require organizations to employ high-profile external experts or industry advisors to assess and identify pricing opportunities within the operations of the company. Through the use of some nonintegrated price experiments or customer surveys, these outside experts often demonstrate the potential benefits of developing pricing capabilities. In many cases, the

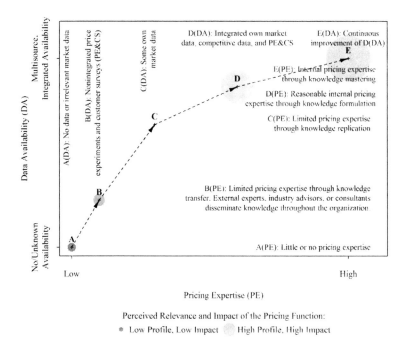

*Figure 2.1. Developing pricing capabilities: Process roadmap.*

knowledge they share with the top management eventually starts to propagate throughout the organization and makes people at all managerial levels aware of the lost revenue opportunities. Yet companies at this stage have limited pricing expertise, as they do not produce but rather transfer relevant knowledge. A typical position for such an organization is point B in Figure 2.1.

Companies that do not feel comfortable knowing that they consistently miss opportunities will typically respond to this threat by heavily investing in technology. In doing so they gain the edge on their slower-moving competitors. The systems that they put in place connect previously uncoordinated organizational functions and provide its users with consistent and high-quality market data. Through mutually beneficial partnerships and agreements with high-visibility pricing and information technology consultants, companies often start to feel and exploit the benefits of their investments shortly after the "go live" system phase. In regard to the internal pricing expertise, however, these organizations are still developing, as they could not yet form their own pricing philosophy to support and drive the business. At best, they now start to replicate what faster-moving competitors have already accomplished in their industry. The lack of highly skilled internal pricing personnel, however, keeps them from capturing all the potential benefits of pricing analytics. Point C in Figure 2.1 is representative of a company at this stage in the development of its pricing capabilities.

Organizations that strive to be predominately analytically market oriented continue to invest in game-changing technology and, equally important, in building strong internal pricing expertise. The integration of their own market data with competitive and alternative sources data is typically complemented by hiring the right people to do the job. The inception of specialized pricing teams within the larger organization is just a normal consequence of this undertaking. As these professionals keep pushing the limits of the organization's information technology (IT) systems, they are now in the position to discover and formulate knowledge. In Figure 2.1 the position of such an organization is at point D.

Point D in our roadmap coincides with the last step of developing pricing capabilities within an organization. To sustain these capabilities and enhance intraorganizational learning, however, the organization needs to continuously invest in improving its market data and data sources and in retaining its best pricing personnel. At this point, the personnel master the skills required in the pricing arena and can use their vast knowledge to run successful industry-wide pricing initiatives. This stage is identified with point E in Figure 2.1. Although it seems that reaching point E is the final goal of a prolonged organizational shaping process, this is rarely the case. In practice, point E as an ultimate final state does not really exist—organizations that complete phases A through D and want to stay ahead of the pack will always be in point E. Hence, successful market-oriented organizations need to continuously fine-tune their pricing approaches and experiment with innovation.

The roadmap depicted in Figure 2.1 shows two other characteristics worth discussing. First, the slight concavity of the broken line that links the developmental points A through E may seem odd. We associate this shape to how we believe most candidate organizations develop pricing capabilities. In particular, the organization's development of internal pricing expertise often lags behind its progress in improving the quality and availability of its data and the sophistication of its IT support systems. Our view acknowledges that quite often the innovation in pricing happens outside of organizations, which use the technology as an enabler for acquiring the needed expertise. Second, the relevance and business impact of the pricing function are often perceived differently by organizations at different stages in the development process. As opposed to organizations at the beginning of their pricing journey, which typically do not fully acknowledge the potential of this function, mature pricing analytics organizations consider it business critical and treat it accordingly. We illustrate this perspective in Figure 2.1 through the use of the radius-varying, color-coded circles that accompany points A through E.

We conclude our discussion of how organizations develop and sustain pricing capabilities by venturing an answer to the questions we posed at the beginning of this chapter. Based on our experience, we believe that it is never too early to start experimenting with pricing analytics. It is our hope that you will find the rest of the material in the book illustrative of how to approach the practical work required by the operationalization of the theoretical concepts. Last, but not least, you should never be satisfied with the progress made—pricing, and more important, successful pricing, is all about being proactive and learning how to identify and exploit each and every revenue opportunity.

## Estimating Price Elasticity

In today's business environment, organizations must often revisit the pricing strategies they put in place when they first introduced their products or services. Changes in the likes and dislikes of consumers, together with competitors' actions, are some of the forces that call for such critical initiatives. Among the questions sellers attempt to answer in these situations, two are consistently at the top of their priority lists. The first relates to whether or not the current prices are aligned with how products or services perform in the marketplace. Since in many cases an unsatisfactory answer is found, the second question focuses on what needs to be done for things to get better. We next provide guidelines on how to navigate the intricacies of such an involved task.

In the marketplace, sellers rarely provide their products or services at an optimized price. Often, offerings are either underpriced or overpriced.

In chapter 1 we explained how to set the optimal prices but deferred the discussion of the details for later. In particular, we have shown how to employ the price elasticity of demand to achieve an optimum price, but we considered the price elasticity a known input into the pricing routine. In reality, however, the price elasticity of demand, as well as the price-response function from which it is derived, is unknown. How does one estimate a sensible price-response function and use it later to infer the price elasticity of an offering? While no definite answers exist, a few general rules apply and can be used to accomplish this undertaking.

Many organizations start this task by specifying a set of possible functional forms for their price-response functions. Usually, this set includes the linear, constant elasticity, or logit specifications, but other more complex forms have also been explored in the literature (e.g., attraction model, Gutenberg model).[2] The price-response functions considered are calibrated using historical data, and the form that describes data the best is typically employed in all subsequent steps, including the derivation of the price elasticity. The calibration of the price-response functions is typically approached by using ordinary least squares or maximum likelihood estimation techniques, which may involve the use of specialized statistical software packages such as R, SAS, or Stata.[3] A short introduction to the software package R, an open source software environment for statistical computing and graphics, is included in the appendix B. At a very high level, the ordinary least squares method minimizes the sum of squared errors among the observed sales and the sales predicted by the calibrated price-response functions. This is the technique used in Microsoft Excel's linear regression function, for example. In contrast, maximum likelihood finds the parameter estimates for the price-response functions such that the probability of the sample data is maximized. In practice, maximum likelihood is typically preferred for estimating most functions, as it is perceived to be more robust and yields parameter estimates with superior statistical properties.

At this point, a typical newcomer to pricing analytics would express at least two points of concern about the feasibility of this approach. On the one hand, relevant historical price/demand data may not be available, as the firm may have consistently priced the product or service at the same level. Alternatively, the firm may operate in a fast-paced environment in which history is not representative of present or future business conditions. Hence, there may be a lack of any calibration relevant market data and data sources. On the other hand, it may be unclear exactly what "describes data the best" means. Fortunately, solutions exist to address both types of concerns.

Organizations that do not have market data readily available to calibrate their candidate price-response functions could rely on price experiments, expert judgment, and/or customer surveys to do so.[4] For example, an online retailer could run a split test on a few representative products in its portfolio to determine the likely response of its customers to various price levels. By randomly diverting the incoming web traffic to product web pages that differ only with respect to the displayed price, the retailer could get an unbiased understanding of how price impacts sales.[5] A word of caution is needed here, as customers who discover that others are receiving lower prices may react negatively against the firm. Thus it is generally better to offer different discount levels off of the same base price during the price experiment (we discuss the psychological aspects of pricing in chapter 5).

Similarly, brick-and-mortar retailers could run in-store price experiments that account for differences among stores to extract the same information from their visitors.[6] If cost or other factors prevent sellers from running price experiments, internal or external experts with good knowledge of the market can be involved to assess how changes in price could impact sales and competitors' reactions.[7] The expert opinion can also be used as a means of validating the results of other pricing initiatives such as price experiments. Some organizations may prefer to estimate price responses by administering surveys to their customers.[8] These surveys may be direct or indirect, paper-based or computer-based questionnaires.

Given the myriad of choices available, how do you choose which ones apply to your particular case?[9] Traditionally, market data price-response functions are considered to be cost efficient since the data are already available, but the range of historical prices charged may not be wide enough to provide accurate price-response function estimates. Expert judgments are perceived as being reliable, accurate, and cost efficient, but the quality is only as good as the experts employed. Price experiments and customer surveys, if sufficiently designed, have been credited with reliability and accuracy but often come at a significant cost. For our take, all options should be considered, and we encourage you to have an in-depth look into your organization's capabilities and core competencies before you commit to any of these choices. Ideally, your ultimate decision should balance such things as the availability and quality of your market data; the extent of your in-house expertise; the types and performance of your revenue and pricing management and customer relationship management systems; and last, but not least, the financial health and potency of your organization. For the remainder of this book, we focus on estimating the price-response functions assuming that some price/demand data are available.

We now proceed with explaining what we mean by choosing the price-response function that describes the data well. To do so, we must be able to quantify how well the price-response functions represent the data. One index frequently employed to judge the quality of this fit is $R^2$ or R-squared.[10] For specifications that promote a linear relationship between sales and price or that can be reduced to such a linear relationship (e.g., the constant-elasticity model), $R^2$ represents the proportion of the variation in sales (or in a transformed measure of sales) that is explained by price. If sales and price were perfectly correlated, then price would fully explain sales, and we would experience a maximum $R^2$ of 1. In contrast, if sales and price were not related or weakly related, we would note an $R^2$ of 0 or close to 0. This is equivalent to saying that sales at various price points are best predicted by the historical average sales and that the historical price offers no additional predictive capability. For the price-response functions for which $R^2$ can be computed, the ones with higher $R^2$ are preferred. Functions that do not support the computation of $R^2$ (e.g., nonlinear price-response functions such as logit) are compared against each other (or against specifications that do support an $R^2$) through the use of different indices such as the *AIC*, or Akaike Information Criterion.[11] The *AIC* attempts to balance the accuracy and complexity of the candidate price-response functions and represents a relative measure. In a practical situation, specifications with lower *AIC*s are preferred. Both measures of fit are part of the standard output of the software packages used to calibrate the price-response functions.

To illustrate how the points mentioned earlier support the overall objective of calculating the price elasticity of demand, in what follows, we briefly discuss case studies of several organizations that have recently gone through relevant pricing initiatives. These examples build on our consulting work and are used here to illustrate the concepts of pricing analytics. We have left out the names of the companies and adjusted some figures to protect our clients' confidentiality. The first organization is a retailer with a significant online presence in the children's products market. The organization has consistently sold one of its representative items in the baby care essentials category at $7.00. At the time of this study, it cost the retailer $2.50 to purchase the item from its suppliers. Customers of this product were believed to respond to changes in price, but the extent of the change was unknown. To investigate whether or not revenue opportunities existed for this product, the retailer ran a price experiment involving multiple price points. In particular, all online customers who accessed the online store during a management prespecified time window were randomly shown product web pages of similar content but different prices. The results of this price experiment are shown in Table 2.2 and graphically depicted in panel A of Figure 2.2. The product manager in charge of this item recommended the price differential of $0.50 based on her experience with the product. To limit lost sales due to inconsistent pricing throughout the period during which the experiment was run, customers who visited the product web page multiple times were consistently shown the same price each time.

The results of the online price experiment were first disseminated within the organization and feedback was requested from all interested parties (e.g., sales and product management personnel). The agreement on the intuitive character of the results was followed by an internal in-depth discussion of the types of price-response functions appropriate for this item. Several functional specifications were explored in connection with the constraints exhibited by the retailer's information systems. The retailer eventually opted for a linear price-response function of the form detailed in equation (1.1). The calibration of this function, that is, the estimation of the intercept $D$ and the slope $m$, was done using the ordinary least squares method for fitting linear models as implemented in R.

*Table 2.2. Online Price Experiment Results*

| Price ($) | 5.0 | 5.5 | 6.0 | 6.5 | 7.0 | 7.5 | 8.0 | 8.5 | 9.0 |
|-----------|-----|-----|-----|-----|-----|-----|-----|-----|-----|
| Sales | 32 | 31 | 30 | 23 | 21 | 21 | 21 | 20 | 13 |

For completeness, we provide a summary of the statistical properties of the parameters of the price-response function and the overall model fit in Table 2.3. These figures suggest that price determines sales following the linear relationship $d(p) = 53.7 - 4.3 \cdot p$, where the intercept $D = d(0) = 53.7$ and slope $m = -4.3$ are both statistically significant and different than 0 at a 99.9% confidence level. The high $t$ *values* (or, alternatively, the small $p$ *values*) support both these conclusions. In this situation, the model predicts that if the retailer prices the product at $0.0, then demand will be 53.7 units of the product. Furthermore, irrespective of the price point charged, the model predicts that if the retailer increases the price by $1.00, then sales will decline by 4.3 units. Based on this linear formulation, any price point above $12.49 is predicted to lead to zero sales. The price-response function seems to fit the data well, as the price alone appears to explain 89% of the variation in sales (see the multiple $R^2$ of 0.89, which is quite close to its maximum value of 1.00). The straight line describing the assumed relationship between sales and price is shown in panel A of Figure 2.2 and superimposed on the experimental sales-price scatterplot.

The characteristics of the price-response function presented in Table 2.3 are unit dependent and, therefore, context specific. To generalize the knowledge and apply it to contexts other than the price experiment itself, the retailer computed the price elasticity of demand across the range of prices with nonzero expected sales. The use of the point elasticity formula for linear price-response functions provided in chapter 1 led to the elasticity curve depicted in panel A of Figure 2.2. At the selling price of $7.00, the price elasticity of demand is in absolute value about 1.28. Armed with this information, the retailer could easily assess the appropriateness

*Table 2.3. Linear Price-Response Function: Summary Statistics and Model Fit*

|  | Estimate | Standard errors | *t value* | *p value* |
|---|---|---|---|---|
| Intercept $D$ | 53.7 | 4.1 | 13.1 | 0.00 |
| Slope $m$ | −4.3 | 0.6 | −7.5 | 0.00 |

Residual standard error: 2.232 on 7 degrees of freedom
Multiple R-squared: 0.89; adjusted R-squared: 0.87
F-statistic: 55.67 on 1 and 7 DF; *p value* : 0.00
Built-in function: lm (R base version 2.11.1)

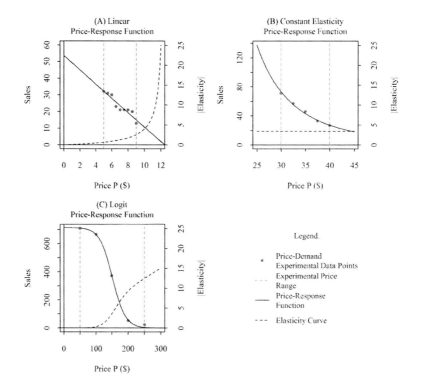

*Figure 2.2. Price-response functions and elasticity curves.*

of its pricing strategy for this product. Following the discussion associated with equation (1.9), it appears that the product was underpriced, as the contribution margin ratio $(p - c)/p$ was less than the reciprocal of the point elasticity $1/\varepsilon(p)$ at the selling price $p$ of $7.00 (i.e., 0.64 vs. 0.78).

Our second example comes from a specialty apparel retailer who operates a small regional network of stores. The retailer sells clothes that target children in their preadolescence stage (i.e., ages 9 to 13) and should appeal not only to the youngsters but also to their legal guardians who typically sponsor the purchases. In an attempt to better understand the likely price/demand relationship for a representative item, the retailer devised and executed a preseason, in-store price experiment intended to capture the price sensitivity of customers shopping for such an item. At the time of the experiment, it cost the retailer $22.00 to purchase the item. The intention of the product managers was to open the season with a product retail price of $34.95, which could later be adjusted based on how the market responded to this initial price. The relatively low gross margin of 37.05% ($12.95) is atypical of the apparel retail industry and reflects conditions relevant to this product only. The experiment was run for a given period of time in a few selected stores that were thought to be representative of the entire chain and accounted for individual store intricacies. The price points at which the product was offered were chosen such that no stores in close proximity featured the product at conflicting prices. Across all stores, the aggregate sales are shown in Table 2.4 and graphically depicted in panel B of Figure 2.2.

As in the case of the retailer in the children's products market, the results of this price experiment were disseminated to all internal groups with an interest in the management of the item. Of these, the fashion merchandise buyers and the marketing and pricing personnel expressed the most opinionated points of view about the observed sales patterns. In particular, while the former group believed that they were appropriately pricing the item, the latter thought that a price increase was needed for the organization to be more profitable. To investigate these claims further, the retailer considered two types of price-response functions to be fitted to the data—with a similar model fit in terms of $R^2$, both linear and constant-elasticity price-response functions constituted good candidate specifications. The linear price-response function was, however, discarded on subjective grounds that had to do with the difficulty of communicating the resulting elasticities to field employees. The retailer felt that communicating a single elasticity for an item would be easier for its less technical employees to grasp.

The calibration of the chosen functional form—that is, the estimation of the constant $C$ and the price elasticity $\varepsilon$ (for details, revisit equation [1.2])—was done using the ordinary least squares method for fitting linear models as implemented in R. To facilitate the calibration, a log transformation was applied to both terms of equation (1.2). This transformation converted the original price-response function to an equivalent but easier to estimate linear specification of the form $\log(d(p))$

Table 2.4. *In-Store Price Experiment Results*

| Price ($) | 29.95 | 32.45 | 34.95 | 37.45 | 39.95 |
|-----------|-------|-------|-------|-------|-------|
| Sales     | 71    | 57    | 46    | 33    | 27    |

$= \beta_0 + \beta_1 \cdot \log(p)$, where $\beta_0 = \log(C)$ and $\beta_1 = \varepsilon$. The recovery of the original function's parameter values comes from $C = \exp(\beta_0)$ and $\varepsilon = \beta_1$. A summary of the parameter estimates, together with the model fit, is provided in Table 2.5. The curve that describes the relationship between sales and price together with the assumed price elasticity $\varepsilon$ is graphically depicted in panel B of Figure 2.2. The $C$ parameter value suggests that at a retail price of $1.00, the organization could sell about 8.7 million units of the product. In the same spirit, the price elasticity $\varepsilon$ of $-3.44$ implies that a 1.00% increase in price is associated with a 3.44% decrease in sales, irrespective of the offered retail price (because it is a constant-elasticity model). For example, by changing the price by 1.00%, from $34.95 to $35.30, the retailer should expect to see a drop in sales of about 3.44%, from 43.28 to 41.82 units (the apparent inconsistencies between the percent and absolute values of the figures are due to rounding errors). The nature of the price elasticity, which stays constant across the full range of prices, helps the retailer determine the quality of its current product pricing strategy. Referring to equation (1.9), we learn that the product seems to be overpriced, as the contribution margin ratio $(p - c)/p$ is greater than the reciprocal of the point elasticity $1/\varepsilon(p)$ at the selling price $p$ of $34.95 (i.e., 0.37 vs. 0.29). This result contradicted the expectations of both groups at the retailer, each of whom thought they had a good understanding of how the product was going to be received in the marketplace.

Over the range of experimental prices, the sales curve $d(p)$ resembles a straight line. Outside of it, a straight line departs significantly from the curvilinear geometry of the constant-elasticity price-response function. In

**Table 2.5. Constant-Elasticity Price-Response Function: Summary Statistics and Model Fit**

|  | Estimate | Standard errors | t value | p value |
|---|---|---|---|---|
| $\beta_0$ | 15.98 | 0.74 | 21.7 | 0.00 |
| $\beta_1$ | −3.44 | 0.21 | −16.6 | 0.00 |
| $C$ | 8,710,154 |  |  |  |
| $\varepsilon$ | −3.4366 |  |  |  |

Residual standard error: 0.05 on 3 degrees of freedom
Multiple R-squared: 0.99; Adjusted R-squared: 0.99
F-statistic: 274.9 on 1 and 3 DF; *p value* : 0.00
Built-in function: lm (R base version 2.11.1)

layman's terms, this means that the differences in behavior between the linear and constant-elasticity price-response functions are expected to be more significant over a larger price range than was covered in the experiment. We illustrate this point by discussing the extreme case of the sales expected to materialize at a price point of $0. For this scenario, the constant-elasticity price-response function we calibrated for the apparel retailer is not satiating and approaches infinity. As this may be too abstract to visualize properly, we reiterate that the retailer is expected to sell some 8.7 million units of the product at a price point of $1.00. In contrast, had the retailer stayed with the linear price-response function, the model would have predicted sales of about 204 units at a price point of $0. The lesson here is that users should be especially wary of using any prediction that is outside of the range of prices the price-response function was estimated on.

The examples we have discussed so far involve the calibration of simple price-response functions. In normal circumstances, any standard statistical software package, including Excel, can be used to complete this task. At times, however, more advanced analytical capabilities are needed to extract relevant insights from the data available. We illustrate this point with an example from a manufacturer who plays an active role in the consumer electronics industry. In the United States, the manufacturer sells its personal digital assistants (PDAs) to end consumers through its own stores or through other retailers such as Wal-Mart and Best Buy. Products can be purchased in the physical stores or ordered online. The competition in the marketplace is fierce for this product type but the prices of competing products have been stable and there are no indications that they will change soon. To prepare for the launch of a new generation model for one of its popular PDAs, the manufacturer ordered an extensive customer survey carried out by an independent, third-party intermediary. Among other things, the objective of the survey was to determine how the market would respond to alternative price points for the product. The survey was administered to existing customers known for their loyalty toward the brand, as well as new consumers who had not historically bought this brand. We present the survey results that are relevant to our discussion in Table 2.6 and panel C of Figure 2.2. These figures, conveniently rescaled to safeguard privacy, are the outcome of a demanding validation effort that required additional inputs from external industry experts, independent consultants, and internal stakeholders with responsibilities in the short- and long-term management of the product. In what follows, we restrict

*Table 2.6. Customer Survey Results*

| Price ($) | 50.00 | 100.00 | 150.00 | 200.00 | 250.00 |
|-----------|-------|--------|--------|--------|--------|
| Sales | 710 | 666 | 373 | 54 | 24 |

the exposition to the calibration of the price-response function(s) and the formulation of price elasticities because the production and research and development (R&D) costs at this manufacturer cannot be disclosed.

The visual inspection of the scatterplot depicted in panel C of Figure 2.2 reveals that an inverse S-shaped price-response function may be appropriate for this product. Although both logit and power functions were considered as qualified candidates, the formulation of price sensitivity measures associated with the former appealed more to the manufacturer. Thus it opted for a logit price-response function that required the calibration of parameter estimates $a$, $b$, and $C$. We performed the calibration using the nonlinear weighted least squares method for fitting nonlinear models as implemented in R. To facilitate the estimation, we rewrote the expression provided in equation (1.4) as

$$d(p) = \frac{C \cdot e^{a+b\cdot p}}{1+e^{a+b\cdot p}} = \frac{C}{1+e^{-a-b\cdot p}} = \frac{C}{1+e^{-(b\cdot p+a)}}$$

$$= \frac{A}{1+e^{-(p-I)/s}} = \frac{A}{1+e^{(I-p)/s}},$$

where $C = A$, $a = -I/s$, and $b = 1/s$. $A$, $I$, and $s$ in this context are geometric elements that carry a palpable meaning. Parameter $A$ represents an upper bound past which sales cannot grow irrespective of the price offered. Similarly, $I$ identifies the price point at the inflection point of the logit curve. Finally, $s$ is a scale parameter on the price dimension. Using R, we first estimated the geometric parameters $A$, $I$, and $s$, from which we derived the values for $a$, $b$, and $C$. A summary of all parameter estimates, together with the model fit, is provided in Table 2.7. In panel C of Figure 2.2, we superimposed the resulting logit curve across the sales-price scatter plot. The $A$ (or $C$) value of 714.56 suggests that sales cannot exceed this value irrespective of the prices offered. At low prices, sales are expected to approach this upper bound and change slowly as the price increases. For example, at a price of $0, sales of about 714.22 units are predicted. The rate of change accelerates as the price increases and reaches its maximum

**Table 2.7. Logit Price-Response Function: Summary Statistics and Model Fit**

|   | Estimate | Standard errors | t value | p value |
|---|---|---|---|---|
| A | 714.56 | 13.1 | 54.5 | 0.00 |
| I | 151.70 | 1.7 | 88.1 | 0.00 |
| S | −19.80 | 1.8 | −10.87 | 0.01 |
| a | 7.66 | | | |
| b | −0.05 | | | |
| C | 714.56 | | | |

Residual standard error: 13.68 on 2 degrees of freedom
AIC: 43.77
Built-in function: nls (R-base version 2.11.1)

value at the inflection point $I = -a/b$ of \$151.70. In business terms, this translates to customers responding aggressively to any price changes made around the market price of \$151.70. Thus small price changes are predicted to lead to significant sales shifts among products and competitors. As prices increase past the inflection point $I$, the curve flattens again and approaches 0 units around a price of \$250.00.

To compute the price elasticity of demand for the logit price-response curve of Table 2.7, we return to equation (1.6), which we rewrite as

$$\varepsilon(p) = \frac{p}{d(p)} \cdot \frac{d}{dp}(d(p)) = \frac{p}{d(p)} \cdot \frac{d}{dp}\left(\frac{C \cdot e^{a+b \cdot p}}{1 + e^{a+b \cdot p}}\right) =$$

$$\frac{p}{d(p)} \cdot \frac{C \cdot b \cdot e^{a+b \cdot p}}{\left(1 + e^{a+b \cdot p}\right)^2} = \frac{b \cdot p}{1 + e^{a+b \cdot p}}$$

or, equivalently, as

$$\varepsilon(p) = -\frac{0.05 \cdot p}{1 + e^{7.66 - 0.05 \cdot p}}.$$

To help provide an understanding of the price elasticity of demand for this manufacturer, the elasticity is plotted in panel C of Figure 2.2. The elasticity increases continuously as the price increases. For example, although the slope of the price-response function at a price of \$250.00 is only −0.25 units per dollar, the ratio of the price and the demand expected to materialize at this price is 50.16. Ultimately, this leads to a point elasticity of −12.54, which is almost two times larger than the elasticity experienced at the inflection point $I$ of \$151.70.

The examples we have discussed up to this point illustrate that the estimation of the price elasticity of demand in practical settings often involves as much art (i.e., subjectivity) as science (i.e., objectivity). As one should be aware of the trade-offs needed when undertaking such a task, we take this opportunity to relate it to the main steps of a typical pricing initiative.

### Step 1: Motivation and Scope

Step 1 is to provide the business logic behind the pricing initiative and clearly identify the project's scope. Scope creep, with a subsequent extension of the project timeline, is a common problem as other areas begin to discover additional business opportunities as the project evolves. Thus clearly defining the scope at the beginning of the project is particularly important. A system-wide, recurrent initiative intended to look into the pricing of thousands of products in real time is li kely to dictate not only the technology to be used but also the pricing analytics embedded in the system's back end. Hence, a balance is needed between the speed and accuracy of the latter to make sure that the system response times stay acceptable.

### Step 2: Design

Step 2 is to look into the roles and tasks of all actors involved with the initiative. Its scope typically drives all decisions at this stage. The choices for technology (e.g., web based); data acquisition and storage (e.g., customer surveys, point of sale data, and enterprise data warehouse, respectively); and pricing analytics (e.g., types of price-response functions) are all influenced by what the organization attempts to achieve. Domain expertise is critical as the links among various project components are not always clear.

### Step 3: Testing

The point of this step is to make sure that the pricing initiative can go live and not experience problems before its actual execution. Few organizations that we have seen skip this step, as it is almost impossible to make things work right from the first attempt. Whether it is unit, integration, or system testing or just survey pretesting, organizations at this stage intend to anticipate, test, and remove obvious or not-so-obvious bottlenecks.

### Step 4: Execution

This step coincides with the "go-live" phase of the pricing initiative. Based on how complex the design is, the execution may take a few days to complete or it may seem to never end. Simple online price experiments focused on the performance of a single product are typically executed in just a few days. Initiatives that are recurrent or designed for continuous performance fall under the latter category.

### Step 5: Control

For pricing initiatives that are recurrent or designed for continuous performance, this step coincides with the maintenance phase. Based on the live performance of the initiative, improvements are often suggested for the original design. However, changes can be expensive to implement and/or can only be partially implemented after the system is in place. Thus it is important to get as much right the first time as possible.

## Estimating Promotion Effects

In many business environments, organizations rely on promotion activities to spur the demand for the products they sell. Retailers, for example, offer their clients a multitude of in-store promotions in an attempt to build store and brand loyalty. "Buy one, get one free," "Now for a limited time only, 25% off," and "Buy one, get the second for 50% off" are just some of the special displays and promo signs that customers expect to see in retail stores. Similarly, in the hospitality industry, hotel chains attempt to improve their occupancies and increase the discretionary spending on hotel-related activities by promising more for less. "Stay four nights and the fifth is on us" is an advertising slogan that is effective for extending the customers' length of stay. Whether communicated to customers as simple temporary price discounts or through a more complex advertising mechanism (e.g., display and feature advertising), these promotions are intended to make up for the reduction in unit margins through an increase in sales volumes. The timing and promotion attributes are usually suggested based on the organization's understanding of its business specificities. At times, however, the complexity of this task overwhelms those in charge with the planning duties and results in unexpected revenue and/or profit losses. For example, it is not unusual for an otherwise carefully designed promotion to lead to out-of-stock (OOS) situations in cases where the promotion effects are underestimated. Similarly, promotions that hurt the bottom line may occur when the effectiveness of related activities is overestimated and the organization is left with high excess inventory. Since success in this case means to be right on target when estimating the promotion effects, in what follows, we refer to several instances that may impede us to do so.

For maximum product exposure, retailers oftentimes offer promotions such that they overlap with periods known for high store traffic. It is not uncommon to walk into Macy's jewelry department days before Mother's Day and notice a sale on all women's jewelry. It is also not uncommon to see this pattern repeat during similar events, including Christmas, Easter, Valentine's Day, and so on. In the absence of other intelligence, this situation may inhibit retailers from differentiating the effect of the price promotion from the normal seasonal effect of the holiday. In this case, whichever effect retailers decide to compute reflects the intrinsic presence of the other one. Hence, the promotion effects are either underestimated or overestimated.

In addition to a possible confounding problem, organizations need to cope with their inability to correctly estimate the true demand for a product or service. To our knowledge, the retail industry faces one of the toughest challenges in this area. As opposed to other industries such as airlines and hospitality, where mechanisms are in place to capture the demand lost due to the product being unavailable, in retail such attempts have proven to be difficult. Typically, the existence of OOS events is not documented, and/or the purchasing intentions of customers facing OOS events are largely unknown. Thus retailers often rely solely on the sales history to infer the product future performance, even though the history may be biased upward or downward by the presence of the same product or other substitutable products' OOS events. In the short term, the downward bias caused by the product stock-outs leads to the retailer underestimating the full potential of promoting the item. In the long term, unless it discovers and adjusts its sales figures to account for this bias, the retailer may experience a dangerous spiral-down phenomenon that could ultimately lead to it being artificially reluctant to promote or assort the item anymore.

Another important factor that impacts the success of a promotion is its timing. For example, organizations that historically promote their fashion-like products close to the end of the season may discover that the same price discounts employed while still in the season may result in significantly higher sales uplifts. This seems intuitive as customers tend to value similar discounts more when the product they purchase is still in fashion. Yet unless organizations experiment to better understand and plan the timing of their promotions accordingly, they will continue to experience recurrent stock-outs or excess inventory.

All else equal, the promotion timing is not the only factor that may lead to undesired results. Quite often, the expectations associated with certain promotions turn out to be unrealistic because no clear differentiation between what contributes to the expected sales uplift exists. For example, the effectiveness of a 25% off promotional offer should be judged on several factors, including the promotional vehicles used to execute it. Yet oftentimes, retailers do not or cannot differentiate among promotional vehicles such as "Now 25% off" or "Buy three, get the fourth free" and plan their promotions unsatisfactorily. In these cases, the retailers' promotion stock levels are frequently amiss.

This digression shows that estimating promotion effects is not a simple task. To add some structure, we present it in the context of the overarching theme of promotion planning and optimization (PPO). Table 2.8 provides a simplified overview of what PPO typically entails. We include the estimation of promotion effects in the Analytical Modeling step and preface an in-depth discussion of what this step requires with a few remarks about its role within the overall PPO framework.

The goal of both the Analytical Modeling and the Validation and Refinement steps is to forecast the likely outcomes of a planned promotion usually at the intersection of three dimensions: product (e.g., blue Hugo Boss stretch jeans), location (e.g., Macy's Herald Square store), and time (e.g., promotion planned for the coming Easter week). To fulfill this goal, insights acquired in time along these dimensions as well as the planned promotion type itself are used. Typically, the promotion histories along the product and location dimensions are first revisited. This effort leads to the estimation of the baseline sales and all other promotion and time-related special events effects. The promotion effects as computed at this stage constitute the basis for the forecast of the results of the planned promotion. They are, however, validated against the historical performance of the planned promotion type across all three dimensions and possibly refined further to account for factors as diverse as their statistical significance, the presence of the planned promotion mix among the historical promotion events, the geographic or time localization of the planned promotion, and so on. In Table 2.8 all data steps that precede Analytical Modeling aim to ensure the accuracy and consistency of aggregate promotion histories at the required product, location, and time dimensions. Similarly, the steps that follow Validation and Refinement are critical, as they ultimately supply and grow the historical collection of promotion effects used in benchmarking and refinement.

Returning to the Analytical Modeling step, the literature on promotion planning and optimization approaches the estimation of promotion effects in two distinct ways. The first way uses data on the promotion histories along the product and location dimensions and attempts to explain individual sales, exposed or not to promotions, via the use of some explanatory variables. Typical explanatory variables are the own and substitutable products' selling prices or its many variants, including percent discount or percent of regular price, the own and substitutable products' promotion types (e.g., feature advertising and/or display), the promotion frequency, the inventory availability (extremely relevant for apparel), the presence of special events such as Christmas and Easter, seasonal variation, and the competitor response. The assumed relationships among sales and the explanatory variables are either additive or multiplicative. Additive relationships operationalized as linear regression models are typically employed when promotion effects are thought to be insensitive to the overall level of the baseline sales. This implies, for example, that under similar promotion conditions, Macy's would expect to sell 20 more pairs of blue Hugo Boss stretch jeans when this item's baseline sales were either 10 or 100 units. Conversely, the multiplicative relationships, log transformed to be operationalized as linear regression models (see Table 2.9), are usually preferred when the promotion effects are considered to be proportional to the absolute values of the baseline sales. Effectively, this

*Table 2.8. Promotion Planning and Optimization*

| 1. Data collection | 2. Data cleansing and storage | 3. Data imputation and aggregation | 4. Analytical modeling[12] |
|---|---|---|---|
| Note:<br>1. POS/scanner data enriched with promo information (e.g., display or feature conditions, advertisement types) and (shelf) out-of-stock intelligence. | Notes:<br>1. Cleanse and permanently store the raw data in the Enterprise Data Warehouse (EDW).<br>2. Typically executed in real time or as a batch process every night. | Notes:<br>1. Impute sales data to reflect own and substitutable products' out-of-stock conditions.<br>2. (Optional) aggregate data to reflect the needs of downstream processes (e.g., daily data to weekly data).<br>3. Typically executed as a weekly or nightly batch process.<br>4. (Optional) employ ETL processes to extract, transform, and load data into external partners' databases. | Notes:<br>1. Employ mathematical models to compute baseline forecasts and promotion and other effects (e.g., discount, special events, and seasonality effects).<br>2. (Optional) compute price elasticity of demand.<br>3. Store results in the Enterprise Data Warehouse.<br>4. Typically executed as a weekly batch process over the most recent relevant promotion histories.<br>5. Some companies outsource this task (see step 3, note 4). |
| 5. Validation and refinement | 6. Promotion planning | 7. Promotion execution | 8. Promotion evaluation |
| Notes:<br>1. Adjust the forecasts and promotion effects based on intimate market knowledge (i.e., query the promotion database in the EDW) or through additional data mining.[13]<br>2. Typically executed together with Step 4. | Notes:<br>1. Order product as per the recommendations of Task 5.<br>2. Order promotion and other support material.<br>3. Communicate to field personnel all required promo details. | Note:<br>1. Execute the promotion. | Notes:<br>1. Analytically evaluate the success of the promotion.<br>2. Store results in the promotion database in the EDW. |

means that a similar promotion effect multiplier of 3.0 applied to Macy's baseline sales of 10 and 100 units would lead to incremental sales of 20 and 200 units, respectively. As we acknowledge that the operationalization of these models is quite subtle, we illustrate them in Table 2.9. In all cases, the estimation of parameter estimates can be done by minimizing the sum of squared errors using the ordinary least squares method.

*Table 2.9. Additive and Multiplicative Promotion Models*

---

### (A) Additive model (Transformation required: None)[14]

General form (linear regression model):

$$Y_t = \alpha + \sum_k \beta_k \cdot X_{t,k} + \varepsilon_t,$$

Example:

$$Sales_t = \alpha + \sum_{k=2}^{K} \beta_k \cdot P_{t,k} + \gamma \cdot SE_t + \varepsilon_t,$$

where $Y$ is the response variable, $X_k$ are the explanatory variables, $t$ is a general index such as time, $\varepsilon_t$ is a 0 mean and constant variance random error term, and $\alpha$ and $\beta_k$ are the parameter estimates that have to be computed from the data.

where $Sales_t$ are the sales during time unit $t$ (e.g., week); $\alpha$ is the average sales at the full price $P_1$ (or the baseline sales); $P_{t,k}$ are indicator variables equal to 1 if at time $t$ price point $P_k$ is offered, 0 otherwise; $SE_t$ is an indicator variable equal to 1 if special events are associated with time $t$, 0 otherwise; $\varepsilon_t$ is a 0 mean and constant variance random error term; and $\alpha$, $\beta_k$, and $\gamma$ are the parameter estimates.

---

### (B-1) Multiplicative model (Transformation required: Natural Log)[15]

General form:

$$Y_t = \alpha \cdot \prod_{k=1}^{K} X_{t,k}^{\beta_k} \cdot \prod_{l=1}^{L} \gamma_l^{X_{t,l}} \cdot e^{\varepsilon_t}$$

Example:

$$Sales_t = \alpha \cdot \left(\frac{P_t}{P_0}\right)^{\beta} \cdot \gamma^{SE_t} \cdot e^{\varepsilon_t}$$

Transformed form (variant of a power model):

$$\log(Y_t) = \log(\alpha) + \sum_{k=1}^{K} \beta_k \cdot \log(X_{t,k}) + \sum_{l=1}^{L} \log(\gamma_l) \cdot X_{t,l} + \varepsilon_t$$

$$= A + \sum_{k=1}^{K} \beta_k \cdot \log(X_{t,k}) + \sum_{l=1}^{L} \Gamma_l \cdot X_{t,l} + \varepsilon_t,$$

Transformed form:

$$\log(Sales_t) = \log(\alpha) + \beta \cdot \log\left(\frac{P_t}{P_0}\right) + \log(\gamma) \cdot SE_t + \varepsilon_t$$

$$= A + \beta \cdot \log\left(\frac{P_t}{P_0}\right) + \Gamma \cdot SE_t + \varepsilon_t,$$

where $Y$ is the response variable; $X_k$ and $X_l$ are the explanatory variables ($X_l$ are typically indicator variables); $t$ is a general index such as time; $\alpha =$ antilog(A); $\gamma_l =$ antilog($\Gamma_l$); $\varepsilon_t$ is a 0 mean and constant variance random error term; and A, $\beta_k$, and $\Gamma_l$ are the parameter estimates that have to be computed from the data.

where $Sales_t$ are the sales during time unit $t$ (e.g., week); $\alpha$ is the average sales at the full price $P_0$ (or the baseline sales); $P_t$ refers to the selling price at time $t$; $SE_t$ is an indicator variable equal to 1 if special events are associated with time $t$, 0 otherwise; $\alpha =$ antilog(A); $\gamma =$ antilog($\Gamma$); $\varepsilon_t$ is a 0 mean and constant variance random error term; and A, $\beta$, and $\Gamma$ are the parameter estimates.

**Table 2.9. (continued)**

---

**(B-2) Multiplicative model (Transformation required: Natural Log)**[16]

| General form: | Example: |
|---|---|

$$Y_t = \alpha \cdot \prod_{k=1}^{K} e^{\beta_k \cdot X_{t,k}} \cdot e^{\varepsilon_t} \qquad Sales_t = \alpha \cdot e^{\beta \cdot (1 - P_t/P_0)} \cdot e^{\gamma \cdot SE_t} \cdot e^{\varepsilon_t}$$

| Transformed form (exponential model): | Transformed form: |
|---|---|

$$\log(Y_t) = \log(\alpha) + \sum_{k=1}^{K} \beta_k \cdot X_{t,k} + \varepsilon_t \qquad \log(Sales_t) = \log(\alpha) + \beta \cdot \left(1 - \frac{P_t}{P_0}\right) + \gamma \cdot SE_t + \varepsilon_t$$

$$= A + \sum_{k=1}^{K} \beta_k \cdot X_{t,k} + \varepsilon_t, \qquad = A + \beta \cdot \left(1 - \frac{P_t}{P_0}\right) + \gamma \cdot SE_t + \varepsilon_t,$$

where $Y$ is the response variable, $X_k$ are the explanatory variables, $t$ is a general index such as time, $\alpha$ = antilog(A), $\varepsilon_t$ is a 0 mean and constant variance random error term, and A and $\beta_k$ are the parameter estimates that have to be computed from the data.

where $Sales_t$ are the sales during time unit $t$ (e.g., week); $\alpha$ is the average sales at the full price $P_0$ (or the baseline sales); $P_t$ refers to the selling price at time $t$; $SE_t$ is an indicator variable equal to 1 if special events are associated with time $t$, 0 otherwise; $\alpha$ = antilog(A); $\varepsilon_t$ is a 0 mean and constant variance random error term; and A, $\beta$, and $\gamma$ are the parameter estimates.

---

The second approach to estimating and subsequently forecasting the promotion effects focuses on promotion events only as the natural promotion planning unit is the promotion event.[17] Its intent is to build accurate predictive regression models by combining all historical promotion events across the product, location, and time dimensions while controlling for diverse factors such as the various variants of the long-term average of the baseline sales, the promotion attributes, the promotion frequency, the presence of special events, and so on. As these models can be calibrated on any promotion data partitions including those temporally driven, this approach seems to be better suited to accommodate the planning of promotions of various durations (e.g., 1 week vs. 2 weeks vs. 3+ weeks).

To see how the promotion effects are estimated in practice, we provide an example of a staple fashion item (e.g., basic denim products such as blue jeans and hosiery) sold by a major retailer throughout the United States. Due to space constraints, we restrict our analysis to 26 weeks of sales as experienced by one of the retailer's stores in the southeast region. Since the promotion events in this sample do not support a thorough discussion of the second approach to estimating the promotion effects, we focus instead on discovering a reasonable relationship between the weekly sales and the available explanatory variables.

The sample spans 6 months of history and covers the period from February to August. In total, four major holidays, including Easter and the Fourth of July, are represented in the data and counted as special events. The item of interest is typically sold at $135.00. At times, to increase store traffic and incentivize customers to purchase, the retailer runs a simple price discount promotion on this item. When offered, the promotion lasts a week at the most. In our sample there are six price discount instances: three relate to a 15% discount and are offered in the spring, while the other three are associated with a 25% discount and are featured in the summer. In four of these cases, the price discounts and the special events overlap. The sales in the nonpromoted weeks are quite stable and average about 59 units per week. The price promotions coupled with the high-traffic special events seem to have a significant impact on sales. Across both of these events, the average weekly sales are 203 units. During the period of study, no OOS events have been reported for this item, so we can assume that the data reflects the true demand. The start of the week inventory is unknown, but it can be assumed that there was enough stock available in terms of sizes for a proper product display. The underlying data are provided in Table 2.10 and graphically depicted in panel A of Figure 2.3.

To estimate the promotion effects, we choose to link the observed sales to the explanatory variables using an additive relationship. Our choice is motivated primarily by the regular patterns noticed in sales

**Table 2.10. Promotion History for a Staple Fashion Item**

| Week | Sales | Price ($) | Special events (SE) | SE indicator | Week | Sales | Price ($) | Special events (SE) | SE indicator |
|------|-------|-----------|---------------------|--------------|------|-------|-----------|---------------------|--------------|
| 1 | 230 | 114.75 | Presidents' Day | 1 | 14 | 50 | 135.00 | | 0 |
| 2 | 71 | 135.00 | | 0 | 15 | 225 | 101.25 | Memorial Day | 1 |
| 3 | 70 | 135.00 | | 0 | 16 | 46 | 135.00 | | 0 |
| 4 | 65 | 135.00 | | 0 | 17 | 51 | 135.00 | | 0 |
| 5 | 60 | 135.00 | | 0 | 18 | 50 | 135.00 | | 0 |
| 6 | 195 | 114.75 | Easter | 1 | 19 | 46 | 135.00 | | 0 |
| 7 | 76 | 135.00 | | 0 | 20 | 253 | 101.25 | Fourth of July | 1 |
| 8 | 51 | 135.00 | | 0 | 21 | 47 | 135.00 | | 0 |
| 9 | 79 | 135.00 | | 0 | 22 | 59 | 135.00 | | 0 |
| 10 | 146 | 114.75 | | 0 | 23 | 55 | 135.00 | | 0 |
| 11 | 69 | 135.00 | | 0 | 24 | 168 | 101.25 | | 0 |
| 12 | 52 | 135.00 | | 0 | 25 | 48 | 135.00 | | 0 |
| 13 | 60 | 135.00 | | 0 | 26 | 73 | 135.00 | | 0 |

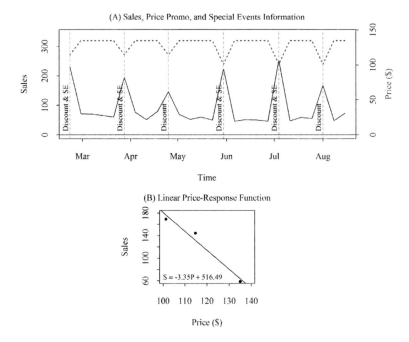

Figure 2.3. *Promotion history for a staple fashion item.*

and the amount of data available. We model the price discount effects through the use of two dummy variables corresponding to the discounted price points of $114.75 and $101.25, respectively. We incorporate the special events effects by using another dummy variable that appropriately identifies the presence of these events. We use the ordinary least squares method for fitting linear models, as implemented in R, to compute all parameter estimates. The estimation results are provided in Table 2.11.

Table 2.11. *Summary Statistics and Model Fit*

|  | Estimate | Standard errors | *t value* | *p value* |
|---|---|---|---|---|
| Baseline sales at $135.00 | 58.9 | 2.7 | 21.6 | 0.00 |
| Price discount $114.75 | 85.6 | 10.3 | 8.3 | 0.00 |
| Price discount $101.25 | 110.6 | 10.3 | 10.7 | 0.00 |
| Special events indicator | 68.8 | 10.5 | 6.5 | 0.00 |

Residual standard error: 12.17 on 22 degrees of freedom
Multiple R-squared: 0.97; Adjusted R-squared: 0.96
F-statistic: 231.6 on 3 and 22 DF; *p value* : < 2.2e-16
Built-in function: lm (R base version 2.11.1)

The price promotion estimates in Table 2.11 suggest that the price discounts do have a significant and differential effect on sales. To this end, a price discount of 15% is estimated to result in incremental sales of 85.6 units. Similarly, a price discount of 25% is estimated to result in incremental sales of 110.6 units. This differential response to the levels of discount offered implies that customers' willingness-to-pay is unevenly distributed across price ranges ($114.75, $135.00) and ($101.25, $114.75), respectively—a valuable insight if the optimization of the product price were attempted. In addition, whenever a special event similar to the ones in the sample takes place, the sales are expected to increase by 68.8 units. From a managerial perspective, this finding is also relevant as high levels of store traffic seem to significantly impact the product's sales at no additional costs. Thus even if no actions are taken to sustainably increase the customer base, rethinking the store product placement may lead to immediate and/or similar incremental gains.

As we already hinted, a special word of caution seems appropriate regarding the differential response to the levels of discount shown in Table 2.11. The price discount effects we have explored so far are all estimated based on a limited promotion history of 26 weeks. Had we considered more of the product history in our exploration, it is quite likely that we would have obtained different results. In addition, our analysis is constrained by the usage of a single type of special events. In practice, however, given the richer information available to your disposal, you may want to differentiate between these events and treat some of them as independent special event instances. It is our expectation that by doing so our price discount effects would have changed as well.

While going through the material presented in this chapter, you may have asked yourself why we had decided to discuss price optimization and promotion effect estimation jointly. There are good reasons to do so, as it is rare for a price/demand dataset to not include some time periods when promotional events occurred. Fortuitously, as long as price variation exists and customers are price responsive, we can usually separate the effect(s) of price on sales from those attributed to other sales contributors such as other promotion attributes, seasonality, special events, and so on. This separation allows for the easy computation of price-response functions appropriate for the dominant market conditions (e.g., no feature advertising or display and no special events). Based on how complex the expressions of these functions are, the price elasticity of demand is subsequently derived either analytically or numerically. Returning to the previous example, we can compute the point estimators of the sales expected to materialize at the three discount levels offered by using the information from Table 2.11. Through simple analytical manipulations, it is easy to show that the expected sales at 0%, 15%, and 25% discount levels are 58.9, 144.5, and 169.5 units, respectively. If a linear price-response function of the form depicted in equation (1.1) was considered appropriate for this application, then the methodology described in the previous section could be employed to yield the following relationship between sales and price: $d = 516.49 - 3.35 \cdot p$. This relationship would ultimately allow us to compute the unit-free elasticity measures needed in a price optimization application. For completeness, we graphically illustrate the sales-price scatterplot together with the linear price-response function in panel B of Figure 2.3.

## Example: Dominick's Finer Foods

Promotions are intended to stimulate sales and capture market share, but with all the complexities involved in making promotional investments, there is a lot of space for making mistakes. To reduce the likelihood of these mistakes taking place or to limit their consequences, retailers need to quantify as precisely as possible the impact on sales of independent or complementary promotion activities. Ideally, a retailer would like to know ahead of time that if a given product gets discounted by 25% in the week of the Fourth of July, sales of the product should increase by five times the normal amount. As an increase of this size may warrant such an aggressive discount level, the retailer could use this information to place an order with the supplier for a quantity that would allow it to satisfy the antici-pated levels of demand. The likelihood of it facing a stock-out and losing revenues and/or profits would therefore be appropriately mitigated. In what follows, we discuss how to sensibly accomplish such a task by look-ing into the operations of a retailer that competes in the grocery industry.

We explore a variant of the model proposed by Foekens et al. (for a relevant overview, see B-1 in Table 2.9) using a subset of the data made publicly available by the James M. Kilts Center, University of Chicago Booth School of Business.[18] The data includes weekly store-level transac-tion prices, quantities, percentage markups, and discount information for more than 100 stores operated by Dominick's Finer Foods, a subsidiary of Safeway Inc., in the Chicago, Illinois, area. Of available products, we focus on the 18 ounce Quick Quaker Oats from the Oatmeal category, sold in the River Forest store during a period of almost 6 years (i.e., June 6, 1991–May 1, 1997). We have selected this product-store pair based on convenience; that is, we have looked specifically for products and stores with consistent sales across an extensive selling window of more than 300 weeks. As no information on OOS situations is available in the data, all weekly records with zero sales are considered stock-out events. This assumption seems reasonable since the total number of zero sales weeks accounts for only 1.9% of the available data. Because the methodology we employ to quantify the promotion effects breaks down when zero sales or price points are present in the data, all such instances have been replaced by the corresponding averages. Other smoothing methods (e.g., median smoothing and moving average) or imputation techniques (e.g., nearest neighbor hot-deck and random hot-deck) can be used to replace missing data with imputed values that are more local in nature.

As per the Dominick's Finer Foods' store zoning of 1992, the River Forest store operated in a high-price tier competitive environment. Throughout the study period, Quick Quaker Oats's regular unit price of $1.99 did not change significantly. The steepest price decrease (vs. price discount) of $0.20 reported for about 8 consecutive months between 1992 and 1993 was followed a year later by a $0.10 price increase that lasted for about 4 months. Various promotion activities, of which some involved price discounts, also altered the product's price for small-time periods. In total, promotions for Quick Quaker Oats were run in 43 of the 309 possible weeks. On average, relative to the closest preceding non-promoted regular price, the product was sold at a 14.9% discount during the promoted periods. The maximum discount was close to 50% and was offered during Labor Day in 1994. Typically, promotions involved various forms of Bonus Buys such as "buy one, get one free" (34/43) and, to a lesser extent, true Simple Price Reductions (9/43). The changes in regular and promotion prices together with promotion timing are depicted in Figure 2.4.

The broken lines shown in Figure 2.4 are illustrative of the relationship between the offered prices and sales. In general, promotions that involve price discounts result in higher than normal sales levels. In addition, higher discounts lead to higher volumes sold. Thus the sales-price

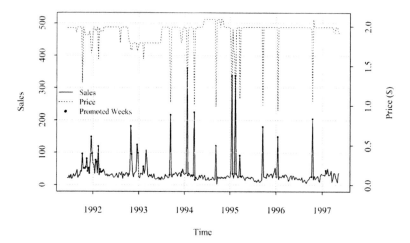

**Figure 2.4. Sales and price plots: Quick Quaker Oats at River Forest store.**

association implied by the power model or its variants (see B-1 in Table 2.9) seems appropriate for this situation. Although the impact on sales of promotion activities tends to mask its presence, a seasonal sales component also appears to exist, which typically peaks during the Christmas/ New Year's Eve time. We study the impact on sales of seasonality through a set of weekly dummy variables. Besides seasonality, the effects of two other sales determinants are explored. The first is special events such as Christmas or Thanksgiving, which are known to influence sales as stores during these periods usually witness elevated store traffic levels. The second is promotion types (e.g., buy one, get one free vs. 25% off). As with seasonality, we employ dummy variables to assess how significant these effects are on the sales of Quick Quaker Oats.

These arguments have prompted us to use the following model specification to compute the promotion effects:

$$S_t = c \cdot \left(\frac{P_t}{\overline{P_t}}\right)^{\beta} \cdot \gamma_l^{D_{t,l}} \cdot \gamma_s^{D_{t,s}} \cdot \left(\prod_{k=1}^{T-1} \delta_k^{X_{t,k}}\right) \cdot e^{u_t}, \qquad (2.1)$$

where $S_t$ are the unit sales in week $t$; $c$ is a constant equal to the base line sales; $P_t$ is the unit price in week $t$; $\overline{P_t}$ is the regular unit price in week $t$ (derived from the unit prices offered during the nonpromoted weeks); $\beta$ is the elasticity of promotional sales with respect to the price reduction ratio;

$l$ identifies a Bonus Buy promotion type; $D_{t,l}$ is an indicator variable equal to 1 if a Bonus Buy promotion is offered in week $t$, 0 otherwise; $\gamma_l$ are the promotion effects associated with a Bonus Buy promotion; $s$ identifies special events such as Thanksgiving and Christmas; $D_{t,s}$ is an indicator variable equal to 1 if week $t$ is a special event, 0 otherwise; $\gamma_s$ is the special event multiplier at the product level; $k$ and $T$ refer to the current season (i.e., week) and the maximum number of seasons (i.e., 52 weeks), respectively; $X_{t,k}$ is a weekly indicator variable equal to 1 if $k = t$, 0 otherwise; $\delta_k$ are the seasonal multipliers at the product level; and $u_t$ is an independent and identically distributed normal error term.

As a preamble to the discussion of how each of the aforementioned determinants impacts sales, it may be worth providing an explanation of the reasons why the multiplicative form of the model shown in equation (2.1) is preferred. In essence, this formulation posits that sales are affected multiplicatively by the discount rates, or equivalently, that the percentage change in sales is proportional to the percentage change in the price discounts. This formulation departs from the theory of the additive models, which provides a proportional relation between the absolute changes in sales and discount levels. From an implementation perspective, this subtle difference provides retailers with maximum convenience. The sales multipliers computed for various discount levels are scale free, simple to understand, and immediately actionable. The same applies to the sales multipliers corresponding to the seasonality, promotion, and special events factors, although these are expressed mathematically in an alternative form. These multipliers are intended to explain the non-price-related variation in sales.

In its current form, the model of equation (2.1) cannot be estimated using linear regression techniques. This being said, it can be converted to a linear equivalent through a log transformation. For example, if we take the natural logarithm on both sides of this model, we obtain a transformed equivalent that is linear in parameters and can thus be analyzed using linear regression. The log transformation yields

$$\log(S_t) = \log(c) + \beta \cdot \log\left(\frac{\overline{P_t}}{P_t}\right) + \log(\gamma_l) \cdot D_{t,l}$$

$$+ \log(\gamma_s) \cdot D_{t,s} + \sum_{k=1}^{T-1} \left(\log(\delta_k) \cdot X_{t,k}\right) + u_t$$

(2.2)

or, equivalently,

$$\log\left(S_t\right) = C + \beta \cdot \log\left(\frac{P_t}{\bar{P}_t}\right) + \Gamma_l \cdot D_{t,l} +$$

$$\Gamma_s \cdot D_{t,s} + \sum_{k=1}^{T-1}\left(\Delta_k \cdot X_{t,k}\right) + u_t. \tag{2.3}$$

In this formulation, the parameters of the multiplicative model can be recovered using the following set of identities: $c = $ antilog($C$), $\beta = \beta$, $\gamma_l = $ antilog($\Gamma_l$), $\gamma_s = $ antilog($\Gamma_s$) and $\delta_k = $ antilog($\Delta_k$).

For Quick Quaker Oats, the parameter estimates for both the log transformed and the original models are shown in Table 2.12. From these results, it is apparent that only the ratio of promoted and regular unit prices and the Bonus Buy promotion significantly impact sales. In addition, certain weekly seasons, relative to the reference week (i.e., Christmas week), lead to significantly differentiated sales levels. To simplify the model, we eliminate the insignificant variables from the full model specification and provide the parameter estimates for the more parsimonious model in Table 2.13. In this case, a 1% decrease in the price ratio is expected to result in a 2.63% increase in sales. Similarly, all else equal, a Bonus Buy promotion is expected to affect sales by a factor of 1.80. The timing of school activities and other major summer holidays appear to also impact sales levels. Relative to other weekly seasons, the end of school in the middle of June (i.e., weeks 25 and 26) leads to a moderate drop in sales. The Fourth of July is also important as the weeks that follow it immediately (i.e., weeks 29–32) all show reduced levels of sales. Finally, the weeks before and after Labor Day, which typically coincide with the end of summer recess (i.e., weeks 35, 36, and 38, respectively), also experience reduced sales volumes.

Armed with these insights, how should the promotion planner prepare for a scheduled "buy three, get the fourth for free" promotion? The model suggests that it depends on the time of the year when the promotion is intended to be offered. If the promotion takes place close to Christmas, for example, then the baseline sales should be adjusted by a multiplier of 2.1 (or $0.75^\beta$) to account for the real price discount and then adjusted by a second multiplier of 1.8 (or $\gamma_l$) to control for the Bonus Buy promotion. In contrast, if the promotion is to be offered in late July, then the resulting multiplier of 3.8 has to be adjusted again by a factor of 0.73 (or $\delta_{31}$) to account for the appropriate seasonality patterns. Now, what if the promotion planner speculates that the computed promotion effects and/or the seasonality profiles are not appropriate anymore for the situation at hand? Even worse, what if she is confronted with a promotion type whose attributes she has not encountered in the past? What if, for example, she is strongly recommended to consider promoting the product using coupons or in-store cart flyers?

First, if it is felt that a product could borrow effects from the product category it belongs to, then the category-level effects on a product holdout sample could be used to assess their forecast accuracy and decide whether or not a substitution is justified. Based on our experience, at times, substituting the own effects for higher-level alternates may lead to significantly better results. This approach, however, requires not only a lot of additional computing power and IT capabilities but also a deep knowledge of how higher-level product groups should be defined. In particular, problems occur when the product hierarchies maintained internally by retailers prove to be impractical to forming the required groups (e.g., jeans, shirts, and boots as a group).

The situations that may require you to consider promoting a product in the absence of any relevant past promotion history can be tackled in a similar fashion. You could attempt to quantify the performance of similar products or groups of products when promoted in this particular way and then borrow and apply this information to your particular case. Alternatively, across all your products and stores, you could link the performance of the promotion type to certain operational characteristics and use the discovered relationship to get an understanding of how the performance of your product could be impacted. Due to the inherent uncertainty that accompanies both approaches, their outcomes are to be expected to be highly variable and certainly less accurate.

## Chapter Summary

We started this chapter with an overview of what developing pricing capabilities within an organization entails. Our graphical roadmap is intended to help identify where your organization is in the process of gaining such capabilities. In close connection to acquiring pricing competence, we stress and stand by the following principles:

- It is never too early to start experimenting with pricing analytics.
- Pricing analytics requires continuous refinement and improvement.

In the first chapter, we showed how price elasticity plays a significant role in the operationalization of pricing analytics concepts. In this chapter, we provide insights into how organizations can go about estimating it. We highlight that selecting the best functional form for the price elasticity curves involves as much science as art. On the science side, one must consider competing functional forms that are calibrated and judged against standard performance metrics. On the art side, one must understand how the business functions and how sophisticated the staff and support systems are. This resource assessment must then be tied to the science of pricing analytics such that an optimal balance is achieved. To provide a possible roadmap, we discuss what a typical pricing initiative requires of an organization and link the estimation of price elasticity to the corresponding upstream and downstream processes.

We next turn our attention to price promotions. Using industries as diverse as retail and hospitality, we examine why promotions are run and what contextual circumstances impede us from accurately estimating the impact promotions have on sales. We provide some proven techniques for estimating promotion effects and discuss these in relation to the overarching theme of promotion planning and optimization. Lastly, we make the connection between the estimation of price elasticity and that of the promotion effects and show how to derive the former from the latter. We conclude the chapter with a case study that illustrates how practical problems can be tackled using the theoretical pricing analytics concepts discussed in the previous chapter.

*Table 2.12. Log-Transformed and Original Multiplicative Models (Full Model)*

| | Log transformed model | | | | Original model | |
|---|---|---|---|---|---|---|
| | Estimate | Standard errors | t value | p value | | Multipliers |
| Intercept $C$ | 3.44 | 0.2 | 17.2 | 0.00 | Intercept $c$ | 31.24 |
| Price ratio $\beta$ | −2.73 | 0.2 | −11.8 | 0.00 | Price ratio $\beta$ | −2.73 |
| Bonus Buy $\Gamma_1$ | 0.50 | 0.1 | 5.8 | 0.00 | Bonus Buy $\gamma_1$ | 1.65 |
| Special events $\Gamma_s$ | −0.05 | 0.1 | −0.4 | 0.67 | Special events $\gamma_s$ | 0.95 |
| Seasonality (Reference: Christmas week) | | | | | Seasonality | |
| ⋮ | | | | | ⋮ | |
| Week 25 $\Delta_{25}$ | −0.43 | 0.3 | −1.71 | 0.10 | Week 25 $\delta_{25}$ | 0.65 |
| Week 26 $\Delta_{26}$ | −0.44 | 0.3 | −1.71 | 0.09 | Week 26 $\delta_{26}$ | 0.65 |
| ⋮ | | | | | | |
| Week 29 $\Delta_{29}$ | −0.62 | 0.2 | −2.5 | 0.01 | Week 29 $\delta_{29}$ | 0.54 |
| Week 30 $\Delta_{30}$ | −0.47 | 0.3 | −1.8 | 0.07 | Week 30 $\delta_{30}$ | 0.62 |
| Week 31 $\Delta_{31}$ | −0.45 | 0.3 | −1.71 | 0.08 | Week 31 $\delta_{31}$ | 0.64 |
| Week 32 $\Delta_{32}$ | −0.45 | 0.3 | −1.71 | 0.08 | Week 32 $\delta_{32}$ | 0.64 |
| ⋮ | | | | | ⋮ | |
| Week 35 $\Delta_{35}$ | −0.67 | 0.3 | −2.6 | 0.01 | Week 35 $\delta_{35}$ | 0.51 |
| Week 36 $\Delta_{36}$ | −0.52 | 0.3 | −2.1 | 0.04 | Week 36 $\delta_{36}$ | 0.60 |
| ⋮ | | | | | ⋮ | |
| Week 38 $\Delta_{38}$ | −0.59 | 0.3 | −2.3 | 0.02 | Week 38 $\delta_{38}$ | 0.55 |
| ⋮ | | | | | ⋮ | |

Residual standard error: 0.3984 on 254 degrees of freedom
Multiple R-squared: 0.64; Adjusted R-squared: 0.57
F-statistic: 8.455 on 54 and 254 DF; $p\ value$ : < 2.2e-16
Built-in function: lm (R base version 2.11.1)

Table 2.13. Log-Transformed and Original Multiplicative Models (Reduced Model)

| | Log transformed model | | | | Original model |
|---|---|---|---|---|---|
| | Estimate | Standard errors | t value | p value | Multipliers |
| Intercept $C$ | 3.31 | 0.0 | 119.7 | 0.00 | Intercept $c$ | 27.29 |
| Price ratio $\beta$ | -2.63 | 0.2 | -12.6 | 0.00 | Price ratio $\beta$ | -2.63 |
| Bonus Buy $\Gamma_1$ | 0.59 | 0.1 | 7.4 | 0.00 | Bonus Buy $\gamma_1$ | 1.80 |
| Seasonality (Reference: All other weeks) | | | | | Seasonality | |
| Week 25 $\Delta_{25}$ | -0.29 | 0.2 | -1.7 | 0.09 | Week 25 $\delta_{25}$ | 0.75 |
| Week 26 $\Delta_{26}$ | -0.30 | 0.2 | -1.8 | 0.08 | Week 26 $\delta_{26}$ | 0.74 |
| Week 29 $\Delta_{29}$ | -0.49 | 0.2 | -2.9 | 0.00 | Week 29 $\delta_{29}$ | 0.61 |
| Week 30 $\Delta_{30}$ | -0.34 | 0.2 | -2.0 | 0.05 | Week 30 $\delta_{30}$ | 0.71 |
| Week 31 $\Delta_{31}$ | -0.32 | 0.2 | -1.9 | 0.06 | Week 31 $\delta_{31}$ | 0.73 |
| Week 32 $\Delta_{32}$ | -0.32 | 0.2 | -1.9 | 0.06 | Week 32 $\delta_{32}$ | 0.73 |
| Week 35 $\Delta_{35}$ | -0.53 | 0.2 | -3.1 | 0.00 | Week 35 $\delta_{35}$ | 0.59 |
| Week 36 $\Delta_{36}$ | -0.39 | 0.2 | -2.3 | 0.02 | Week 36 $\delta_{36}$ | 0.68 |
| Week 38 $\Delta_{38}$ | -0.46 | 0.2 | -2.7 | 0.01 | Week 38 $\delta_{38}$ | 0.63 |

Residual standard error: 0.4107 on 297 degrees of freedom
Multiple R-squared: 0.56; Adjusted R-squared: 0.54
F-statistic: 33.78 on 11 and 297 DF; $p\ value: < 2.2e\text{-}16$
Built-in function: lm (R base version 2.11.1)
Note. The special events indicator variable together with other 42 seasonal indicator variables is removed from the full model specification.

# CHAPTER 3

# Dynamic Pricing and Markdown Optimization

The last few years have witnessed a significant change in how organizations have approached the pricing of their products and services. Slowly but surely more and more companies have embraced and promoted dynamic pricing as a means of meeting the needs of individual customers and dealing with particular business situations. News reports in the popular media and articles in the scientific press have highlighted the potential benefits associated with dynamic pricing. A quick scan of these sources reveals that the concept has already crossed industry boundaries and has become the *new thing* in industries as diverse as utilities (e.g., Pacific Gas and Electric Company, a subsidiary of PG&E Corporation), ticketing (e.g., Digonex Technologies Inc.), and the arts (e.g., the Arts Club Theater Company in Vancouver). These featured success stories help build excitement for the science of dynamic pricing, but they often lack the depth or conciseness that one needs to really understand it. In this chapter, we answer the questions "What is dynamic pricing?," "What are the most popular forms of dynamically pricing a product or service?," and "How can you implement it and exploit its benefits?" We start the chapter by providing an understanding of what dynamic pricing is and what it entails. We then delve into the details of markdown optimization, which is one the most practiced forms of dynamic pricing. Finally, we conclude the chapter with a discussion of a few relevant real-life examples.

## Dynamic Pricing

Parties involved in commerce have experimented with variable pricing since the beginning of commerce itself. Throughout history, most transactions between sellers and buyers have involved some form of bargaining. In some Middle East cultures, bargaining became such a social phenomenon that not being open to negotiate was often taken as a great offense. Based on who had the bargaining power, buyers and sellers would typically agree on a selling price that was perceived to be fair by both parties. Yet had the business circumstances or the control of power been different, the same buyers and sellers may have reached agreements of a different nature.

Throughout the 20th century, with the development of the modern retailing in the Western societies, the focus of pricing has shifted from variable to static pricing. The diversity of the product assortment and the variety and size of the customer base made it difficult for retailers to sustain any viable variable pricing initiatives. Today, the "one-size-fits-all" approach in terms of pricing has become the norm in many business-to-consumer (B2C) industries. Typically, the reluctance of organizations to adapt to market forces and adopt alternative pricing strategies has been linked to the high costs of physically changing prices and/or acquiring the required sophisticated hardware and software support platforms. Imagine, for example, that a Wal-Mart Supercenter had the capability to compute daily a set of highly accurate prices for all its hundreds of thousands of products. In spite of its accuracy, the execution of such a price change would require an organizational effort that store managers could not afford. Hence, they would disregard most, if not all, of the price recommendations. However, if in-store electronic shelf labels were available, the likelihood that the same store managers would accept and implement the suggested price changes would be substantially increased.

In some business contexts, however, the static trends in setting and maintaining prices have been challenged and reversed for quite a while. In these environments organizations attempt to update the prices of their products or services continuously based on market forces including the foreseen demand, the supply availability, and other contextual factors such as seasonality and special events. In our view, dynamic pricing refers to this process of continuously adjusting the prices to meet the evolving needs of the organization and its customers. Although from the outside the process seems to be controlled primarily by sellers, in practice, it does involve some subtle forms of bargaining where, at times, buyers gain control. For example, when the needed supply is overestimated, sellers tend to lower prices to spur the demand for their products or services and clear the excess inventory. In informal terms, sellers admit that they have made a purchasing, allocation, or replenishment mistake and intend to correct it by inviting buyers to purchase at discounted prices. In this case, buyers are in control as their tardy response may trigger other subsequent price discounts. In contrast, when the available supply is perceived as insufficient, smart sellers may increase the price in anticipation of the elevated levels of demand. Their message to the customers could very well be summarized as, "We know we have a valuable asset and we are more than happy to share it with you as long as you are willing to pay the right price for it." Obviously, sellers own the negotiation power in this case. We have brought up the discussion of who is in control of what and when simply to illustrate how dynamic pricing functions. In reality the shift in control, although real, happens seamlessly without any explicit reference to its existence. The bargaining, that is, the decisions of when to change the price and by how much, is typically controlled in the background by sophisticated and costly algorithms that utilize information gathered from various sources to offer their price recommendations.

The answer on who exactly originated the modern form of dynamic pricing is not simple as the literature does not seem to share an unequivocal perspective on this issue. Some authors have credited airlines and hotels as being the first to engage in dynamic pricing.[1] Others have considered the pioneering efforts of these organizations as the precursors of the modern dynamic pricing.[2] These differences aside, airlines and hotels in late 1970s started to ration the availability of their supply in an attempt to become more market oriented, more responsive, and more profitable. By limiting customers' access to classes of products priced distinctively, these organizations often seemed to be engaged in dynamic pricing. The apparent price changes, however, were exclusively due to the allocation of available capacity to the underlying product classes and not to a conscious effort of recalculating prices. Hence, sales were controlled by appropriately allocating the capacity and not by optimally setting the prices. This subtle difference sparked the debate in the literature over which firms really employ dynamic pricing. Nowadays, fueled by the fierce competitive environment and fickle customer base, both airlines and hotels seem to have moved toward operations that more closely resemble dynamic pricing than capacity allocation. InterContinental Hotels Group and Carlson Hotels Worldwide, for example, have claimed to have the capability of optimizing the retail rates at all participating hotels in their portfolios in real time based on consumer response, competitive rates, and capacity constraints.[3]

The encouraging results experienced by airlines and hotels prompted organizations in other industries to start experimenting with dynamic pricing. Retailers of style and seasonal goods such as Gymboree and Bloomingdale's looked at it as an opportunity to better manage the demand and control the losses due to out-of-stock (OOS) events, lost sales, and excess inventory. Since in-season product replenishment is not a viable option for many fashion retailers, they have to make the most out of a fixed inventory. Typical dynamic pricing strategies employed by these retailers are the preseason price promotions and the in-season temporary and permanent price markdowns. In contrast, retailers of nondurable goods, such as Safeway and Walgreens, face the pressing question of how to manage pricing and replenishment together such that decisions in one area support those in the other. For example, offering a product in short supply at a low price could be detrimental as the corresponding sales rates would likely lead to OOS events and lost revenue opportunities. Based on customers' price sensitivity, a better alternative could be to temporarily increase the price in anticipation of the arrival of a new product batch. In spite of the potential of coordinating pricing and procurement, dynamic pricing by nondurable goods retailers is still rare. Instead, most retailers resort to category or product hierarchy–grouping pricing to frequently adjust the regular product prices in the absence, though, of any inventory-related information.

One would be remiss to review the field of dynamic pricing without referring to what it involves in e-business environments (firms selling primarily through the Internet). In particular, e-business seems to be the most natural host of dynamic pricing applications due primarily to two intertwined developments.[4] First, the online medium supports the seamless transfer and circulation of information through the entire business. Any price changes recommended by the analytics engines or suggested via human interventions are now propagated instantaneously through the information technology (IT) system network. Thus the high costs of physically changing the posted prices are no longer an issue in the context of e-businesses. Second, the prospects of an increased customer base have been associated with an increase in the uncertainty and composition of demand, which in itself is expected to warrant the use of dynamic pricing. In particular, it has been speculated that in online markets, static prices are both ineffective and inefficient. We refer next to a few issues that online markets promise to deliver on.

Technological advances exploited by service providers in the online customer relationship and experience management domains allow e-businesses to collect customer data at an unprecedented level of detail. Software applications such as those provided by CoreMatrix LLC or Tealeaf Technology Inc., among others, enable online businesses to find and remove inconsistencies in their virtual store designs, track customers' interaction with these stores, and last but not least, learn the search and purchase behavior of their customers. These features facilitate the development of customized pricing where it is now feasible for each online customer to be quoted her own retail price. If the current trends continue, it is not unrealistic to believe that these customized prices could be further refined in real time to dynamically account for other contextual factors including inventory levels, day of week, time of day, customer worthiness, and the prices at competitors. Although built on different needs and principles, Priceline.com provides a relevant example of where dynamic/customized pricing is today in online environments. Among other services, the company allows its customers to name their own prices for opaque travel services, that is, services acquired from providers but presented to the customer with an unknown service time or provider's identity. In this case, last-minute travelers looking for a deal could benefit from the distressed inventory of organizations that likely wouldn't have otherwise sold it. As each offer is customer-specific and accepted if a minimum profit margin is guaranteed, Priceline.com's practices can be viewed as providing customized pricing at close to the customer's willingness to pay.

Given the advantages of dynamic pricing mentioned previously, why have not more organizations and industries rushed to embrace and practice it? In addition to the reasons we have already hinted at, there are quite a few others that may prevent companies from experimenting with it. Take, for example, the case of retailers in the luxury item business. Although at times they may experience weak demand, they tend not to rely on any price discounts to accelerate sales as such an approach would diminish the value of their brands and anger their loyal customers. For example, a collector who invested $200,000 in a Patek Philippe wrist-watch would not like to see her collection item being sold for $10,000 at another time or place. Alternatively, some organizations' missions may conflict with the for-profit concepts popularized by dynamic pricing. An opera house or an arts center that desires to make their product accessible may have a hard time explaining to its donors and supporters that dynamic pricing helps it survive. Lastly, companies that employ dynamic pricing may lose their credibility as customers confronted with changing prices for products they perceived undifferentiated may feel cheated. To avoid such a reputation, airlines and hotels, for example, clear their excess inventory through online travel aggregators (e.g., Expedia.com) or opaque channels (e.g., Priceline.com) rather than through their own websites. In doing so, last-minute travelers adamant to catch specific flights or stay in particular hotels are continued to be charged regular prices without feeling exploited.

Whether you need to clear your excess inventory or set up and adjust the prices for your products or services to reflect the changing needs of your organization and customers, dynamic pricing may help you do it more profitably. At a high level, it intends to replace the gut feeling approach to doing business with fact-driven decision making. The required facts are typically derived and learned from customer data and updated regularly as markets evolve. From our experience with dynamic pricing systems, successful organizations start their implementation journeys small but with very aggressive deadlines. Prototypes developed in house or with external assistance that prove the feasibility of the concept and prepare the organization for it are usually followed by a fast and furious full-scale roll out. Since implementations often cost millions of dollars, the rush to deliver the systems is understandable—the management team will be eager to start enjoying the benefits of its investment as quickly as possible. How the journey ends is often a reflection of (a) how supportive of the project the upper management is, (b) how experienced the project management team is, and (c) how diligent and knowledgeable the implementation team is. To help fully understand the implications of these three success pillars, we paraphrase a saying from the tough world of mountaineers: "You can attempt to conquer Everest if you have some money, a good plan, and an excellent companion. Nothing else seems to work."

# Markdown Optimization

In this section we focus on retailers of style and seasonal goods who at times may need to offer permanent in-season price markdowns in an attempt to spur sales, clear excess inventory, and maintain healthy margins. In many cases, moving the excess inventory off the sales floor fast and at high margins is the number one explanation for why retailers employ price markdowns. Judiciously planning these activities, however, is not an easy task as the pricing decisions made at any one stage in the lifetime of a product tend to be irreversible and could impact the bottom line dramatically. On the one hand, aggressive markdowns may clear the excess inventory fast but could hurt margins as the marketplace could accept higher prices. On the other hand, conservative markdowns may lead to unsold inventory that could require deep price discounts to clear at the end of the season. In what follows, we look into the specifics of price markdowns primarily with respect to how they connect to the problem of clearing the excess inventory. While such considerations have been often linked to why retailers are forced into offering markdowns, we add to this perspective by briefly referring to other alternative explanations.

One of these builds on the fact that style and seasonal goods retailers experience long lead times and operate in highly uncertain environments. It is not unusual to take such a retailer as long as 9 months to have its new products delivered in stores. In addition, during the ordering lead time, past trends in customer preferences may change dramatically leading to retailers bearing a high obsolescence risk. Popular quotes such as "In fashion apparel, there is nothing as boring as last season's hot sellers" are illustrative of the seriousness of the problem.[5] Hence, to manage demand uncertainty and stay profitable, retailers tend to introduce their products to the market at high margins. For example, percentage gross margins as high as 85% are customary in fashion apparel. Of the products on the selling floor, items perceived trendy by customers sell well throughout the season and do not need any special intervention. Slow moving items, however, which in the eyes of the customers may appear unjustifiably overpriced, tend to lag behind the financial objectives and are typically considered good candidates for markdowns. In this situation markdowns can be looked at as mechanisms of demand learning.[6]

Another perspective on what contributes to markdowns being offered sees an item as a time-dependent collection of attributes. Specifically, it suggests that the same physical item is worth more or less based on when in the season the purchase intention is expressed. Thus it implies that, throughout the season, such an item could appeal to customers with different price sensitivities. A spring season Miss Cristo cork sandal featured on the catwalk of the New York Fashion Week in September may appear on the shopping list of many shoe lovers. Yet only those who perceive the item as a must-have will subject their wallets to the premium price of $595 to get it in the preseason. The rest, however, who cannot afford it or may value it at a lower price, may prefer to postpone their purchasing decision, hoping to get it at a lower price. Markdown pricing is perceived in this context as a segmentation mechanism intended to differentiate between customers with different price sensitivities.

Our digression, while informative, sheds little light on the problems associated with price markdowns. In particular, you could ask why we should care about markdowns at all. In the absence of any other support material, you could even question our choosing to discuss this topic distinctively from the overarching theme of dynamic pricing. Well, it turns out that there are good reasons for us to stick to our plan. To help you get the feel for the types of problems markdowns may lead to, we adapt the example of the staple fashion item introduced in the previous chapter to suit our current needs. For simplicity, let's suppose that the item whose regular retail price is $135 is a seasonal item that costs $35 to procure from the manufacturer. The retailer would practice in this case a percentage markup of 285.7% and a percentage gross margin of 74.1%. Now, let's further consider that the item does not sell well and the retailer is tempted to mark it down to a new retail price of $100. The price slash means a recalculated percentage markup of 185.7% and a percentage gross margin of 65.0%. In this case, the 9.1% gross margin contraction reflects the $35 nominal markdown. Now, let's suppose that the retailer sells 10 units of the item at the markdown price of $100 and makes $1,000 in sales. The disturbing reality is that while it has made $650 in profits, the retailer has still lost $350, or 35% of the actual sales, due to markdowns.

We build on this admittedly extreme example and illustrate the prevalence of markdowns in the modern era using the case of U.S. department stores. Based on the financial and operating results published by the National Retail Federation, U.S. department store markdowns more than tripled between 1971 and 1997 and reached an all-time high of close to 30% of sales in 1996.[7] To illustrate the gravity of the problem further, we refer to the recent case of Sears Holdings Corporation, which reported a 2008 first-quarter net loss of $56 million that they attributed to the weak retail environment and, equally important, markdown-related gross margin contractions intended to move inventory.[8] In spite of the overwhelming evidence that price markdowns are to be avoided, retailers do it customarily and there are no signs that the practice will go away any time soon. So why are markdowns offered? Are they really needed and, if so, how should they be handled?

In the last decade, the worrying proliferation of price markdowns has been associated with the product customization required by a fickle customer base. In particular, the product range flexibility as reflected in the styles, colors, and sizes assorted has commoditized and become a qualifying competitive factor rather than an order-winning one. This shift has forced style and seasonal goods retailers to respond to the changing market requirements by assorting more and more products often only marginally differentiated. This in turn has led to a highly uncertain environment in which retailers have been more susceptible to make mistakes along their entire supply chain (e.g., forecasting, product assortment, purchasing, store allocation, and pricing). The boost in the utilization of markdowns is hypothesized to be the result of retailers not being able to cope with the increased uncertainty prevalent in their business environments.[9] For these reasons, in fashion apparel, for example, it is quite infrequent that styles perform as per their financial objectives. Some sell out before the end of the season while others, stocked in substantial amounts, do not sell at all or sell poorly. In the absence of any initiatives to stimulate demand, this slow-moving inventory is likely to go obsolete at the end of the season and be salvaged at no or little profit. Markdowns in this case are intended primarily to clear this type of inventory. They too generate cash to be used to assort other better-selling products. Last but not least they create store excitement and increase traffic and sales of complementary products.

Up to this point we have stressed the idea that markdowns are not to be practiced if at all possible. Along these lines, retailers able to identify slow-moving inventory early in the season may have the option to exchange or return the corresponding products to the supplier. We have also emphasized that oftentimes markdowns are to be taken as they are the last resort to making profit from a sunk inventory investment. In most cases, retailers approach this task statically. Some employ extensions of the Filene's Basement automatic markdown system and offer markdowns based on the time the product spends on the shelf—for example, 25% off after 4 weeks, 50% off after 8 weeks, 75% off after 12 weeks, and charity donation after 16 weeks. Others monitor product performance continuously and identify slow moving items that do not sell as per the expectations. Items that consistently lag behind are typically marked down during predetermined end-of-season clearance periods, which, in some instances, may last up to 3 months. In the markdown periods, qualified items are sold at various time-dependent price points (e.g., 25% off, 50% off, 75% off, multiple of $5 but less than 70% off) until all excess inventory is cleared. These prolonged clearance events, while effective in getting rid of the obsolete inventory, do tend to interfere with customers' in-store experience as the introduction of new collections overlaps the massive clearance events. Esprit, V&D, and Zara all practice this markdown style in parts of Western Europe. To try not to let clearance activities spoil the in-store customer shopping experience, some retailers with e-presence run these events exclusively online. Others, such as Nordstrom through its Nordstrom Rack chain of stores, prefer to consolidate the in-season leftover merchandise at central locations where they attempt to mark it down collectively and profitably sell it.

In recent years some retailers, including Bloomingdale's and Gap, have started experimenting with dynamic in-season markdown policies. Both retailers have come to realize that the static approach to marking down prices is too limiting in that it promotes the clearance of inventory in the absence of any sound considerations on how margins are impacted. Hence, they have started to rely on optimization software packages to compute the optimal timing and depth of the proposed markdowns with the explicit goal of maximizing gross margins. These systems use the up-to-date in-season product performance together with the continuously adjusted season forecasts to analyze competing pricing scenarios and recommend appropriate markdown policies. The benefits of employing dynamic markdown pricing are expected to justify the high capital costs associated with a full-scale system implementation. For example, Oracle, one of the software vendors with a significant footprint in the retail industry, estimates that its markdown optimization solution contributes to a 5%–15% increase in its customers' gross margins.[10] Similarly, AMR Research, now part of Gartner Inc., considers that markdown optimization initiatives have the potential to add 6%–10% to an organization's gross margins.[11]

# Examples

In this section we provide some insights into how price markdowns are often approached in practice. The first example builds on the concept of slow-moving items and illustrates how to identify profitable markdown opportunities. The second example uses linear programming to solve a simple markdown optimization problem in which revenue maximization is considered explicitly.

## Price Markdowns and Slow-Moving Items

Given the significant number of products that they routinely assort, retailers tend to track the in-season performance of their merchandise in an attempt to identify timely items that are likely to over- or underperform. Often, this effort is undertaken for buyers and supply chain managers to be able to react to the current market conditions. For style and seasonal goods retailers, an overperforming item often results in missed revenue opportunities as the long order lead times often impedes any effort to restock the item. In contrast, items that underperform the market expectations are monitored closely as there is a high likelihood for them to go obsolete, requiring salvaging the item at no or little profit. Most retailers physically review these items to get an understanding of what seems to cause the customer distress and then decide which items to mark down. Current practices require pricing managers to wait in their assessment until the item introductory period is considered complete. It is not uncommon in the fashion apparel retail industry, for example, to compute the first slow-moving indices after observing 6 weeks of demand from the time the item was first introduced. If the introductory period is too long, however, the markdown of an item could take place at times when customers' interest for it is considerably reduced (e.g., end-of-season clearance events).

We propose that either no or minimal restrictions be placed on when slow-moving indices are computed. If discovered fast enough, some retailers may have an opportunity to exchange or return these items to the supplier. For a full coverage of this and other related topics, we encourage the savvy reader to consult the material discussed in Walker.[12]

To begin our example, suppose that a retail store starts its 16-week fall season with 1,000 pairs of seasonal Hugo Boss New Wave jeans in stock. For such items, the retailer usually plans for a desired maximum end-of-season percentage inventory $f_n$ of 0.15 (or, equivalently, 150 pairs). The season has started strong with reported sales for the first 2 weeks of 100 and 75 pairs, respectively. Based on this limited information, the retailer intends to assess the product performance and start thinking of alternative selling strategies if sales are not satisfactory. At first glance, it may appear that there are no good reasons for the retailer to worry about the sales performance of this product for the remaining of the season. This would be a reasonable assumption if the sales trend stays the same; the retailer is projected to be out of stock before the end of the 12th week. But what if the trends change? What if customer excitement for this item deteriorated as the season progressed? How should the retailer respond to this scenario, and, equally important, what should the magnitude of its response be?

It turns out that in the absence of any reliable historical-based forecasts, the retailer could still compute an end-of-the-season inventory estimate from limited in-season available data. In particular, one approach routinely employed by retailers of style and seasonal goods involves discounting the end-of-a-period inventory $I_j$ by an inventory proportionality factor $F_c$ assumed to stay constant until the end of the season. Following the notation in Walker for consistency, we can write the forecast for the end of the season inventory at the end of period $j$ as

$$i\left(n, I_j, I_0, F_c\right) = I_j \cdot \underbrace{F_c}_{(j+1)} \cdot \underbrace{F_c}_{(j+2)} \cdots \underbrace{F_c}_{(n)} = I_j \cdot \left(F_c\right)^{n-j},$$

where $I_j$ is the available inventory at the end of period $j$, $n$ is the length of the selling season (e.g., 16 weeks), and $F_c$, bounded by 0 and 1, is the inventory proportionality factor current at time $j$. $F_c$, expressed as

$$\left(\prod_{k=1}^{j}\left(I_k/I_{k-1}\right)\right)^{1/j}$$

or, equivalently, $(I_j / I_0)^{1/j}$, is the geometric mean of the period-to-period less than unit growth rates that accompany the move from $I_0$ at the start of the season to $I_j$ at the end of the $j$th time period. Stated otherwise, this forecasting method derives an average period-to-period inventory proportionality factor from the observed sales and uses it to discount the most current end-of-the-period inventory levels to account for the length of the remaining selling season. H. B. Wolfe conducted an extensive study of fashion items in several women's clothing departments and provided the empirical basis for this forecasting approach.[13]

Returning to the example of our retailer, we have enough information to compute the end-of-the-season inventory forecasts after the sales for the first and second weeks are reported. Our analytical steps are summarized later and reveal that the item maintains a slow-moving status at the end of both weeks. If trends do not change significantly in the near future, the retailer may need to find alternative ways of accelerating sales, potentially through price markdowns. For illustration purposes only, we also refer to the hypothetical case when 125 pairs of jeans are sold in the second week. With only 775 units in inventory at the end of the second week, the item changes status to a regular selling product that, at least for now, does not require increased monitoring:

Week 0: $I_0 = 1{,}000$,

Week 1: $I_1 = 900$; $F_c = (I_1/I_0)^{1/1} = 0.90$; $i = I_1 \cdot (F)^{n-1} = 900 \cdot (0.90)^{15} = 185.3$
$i = 185.3 \geq f_n = 150$ (Status: Slow-Moving Item),

Week 2 (Actual): $I_2 = 825$; $F_c = (I_2/I_1 \cdot I_1/I_0)^{1/2} = 0.91$;
$i = I_2 \cdot (F)^{n-2} = 825 \cdot (0.91)^{14} = 214.6$
$i = 214.6 \geq f_n = 150$ (Status: Slow Moving Item),

Week 2 (Hypothetical): $I_2 = 775$; $F_c = (I_2/I_1 * I_1/I_0)1/2 = 0.88$;
$i = I_2 \cdot (F)^{n-2} = 775 \cdot (0.88)^{14} = 130.1$
$i = 130.1 \leq f_n = 150$ (Status: Regular Item).

Assume now that the retailer takes these early warnings seriously and intends to mark down the price of the item to spur sales. The retailer's intuitive decision to cut the selling price, however, triggers a series of subsequent decisions that are slightly more difficult to handle. In particular, the retailer needs to investigate if the item qualifies for a markdown and, if so, when and by how much should the price be reduced. On the one hand, if there are no legally binding agreements with the manufacturer to preserve the image of the brand through consistent pricing, the retailer can attempt to lower the price. On the other hand, if it does so, it needs to do it such that the markdown is economically viable. In what comes next, we focus on this latter task of deciding what markdowns are viable at each particular moment in time.

The immediate effect of the retailer's decision to markdown, at the end of period $j$, the unit price from, say, $P_c$ to $P_m$ should be a marginal increase in the sales of period ($j + 1$). If $S^c_{j+1}$ and $S^m_{j+1}$ are the expected sales at $P_c$ and $P_m$, respectively, then $S^m_{j+1} - S^c_{j+1} \geq 0$, or, equivalently, $(I_j - I_j \cdot (F_m)^1) - (I_j - I_j \cdot (F_c)^1) \geq 0$. $F_m$, in this expression, is an unknown inventory proportionality factor associated with the unit price being marked down from $P_c$ to $P_m$. Similarly, $I_j \cdot (F_m)^1$ and $I_j \cdot (F_c)^1$ are the end-of-period ($j + 1$) inventory forecasts in the presence of a unit price of $P_c$ and $P_m$, respectively. Subsequent algebraic operations applied to the expression of incremental sales lead to $F_c \geq F_m$, which is a necessary but insufficient condition to justify the markdown economic viability.

To uncover sufficient conditions that would warrant a markdown, we link the discussion of the incremental sales for period ($j + 1$) to the revenues expected to materialize during the remaining of the selling season, or ($n - j$) time periods. At the full price $P_c$, the retailer is expected to sell items worth $P_c \cdot (I_j - I_j \cdot (F_c)^{n-j})$, or $P_c \cdot I_j \cdot (1 - (F_c)^{n-j})$. By the same logic, the revenues to be experienced at the markdown price $P_m$ can be expressed as $P_m \cdot (I_j - I_j \cdot (F_m)^{n-j})$, or $P_m \cdot I_j (1 - (F_m)^{n-j})$. In these circumstances, the item is considered economically viable for a markdown if and only if the revenues expected to materialize at the markdown price $P_m$ equal or exceed those expected to be experienced at the full price $P_c$. In formal terms, this translates into

$$P_m \cdot I_j \cdot (1 - (F_m)^{n-j}) \geq P_c \cdot I_j \cdot (1 - (F_c)^{n-j}), \text{ or}$$

$$1 - (F_m)^{n-j} \geq \frac{1 - (F_c)^{n-j}}{P_m/P_c}. \quad (3.1)$$

As an aside, note that in equation (3.1), $F_m$ is bounded by 0 and 1. This necessarily means that an economically viable markdown exists if and only if $P_m/P_c > 1 - (F_c)^{n-j}$.

The expression in equation (3.1), while informative of how an appropriate markdown policy should be approached, is difficult to operationalize as $F_m$ is unknown. In the absence of any reliable historical estimates for $F_m$, the retailer can build on equation (3.1) to get

$$F_m \leq \left(1 - \frac{1-\left(F_c\right)^{n-j}}{P_m/P_c}\right)^{1/(n-j)}. \tag{3.2}$$

Using the formulation of expected sales for the end of period $(j+1)$ in the presence of both $P_c$ and $P_m$, the expression can be rewritten as

$$\frac{S_{j+1}^m}{S_{j+1}^c} = \frac{\left(1-F_m\right)\cdot I_j}{\left(1-F_c\right)\cdot I_j} \geq \sigma\left(j,n,P_m/P_c,I_j/I_0\right) =$$

$$\sigma(.) = \frac{1-\left[1-\dfrac{1-\left(I_j/I_0\right)^{(n-j)/j}}{P_m/P_c}\right]^{1/(n-j)}}{1-\left(I_j/I_0\right)^{1/j}} \tag{3.3}$$

to link the expected sales ratio $S_{j+1}^m / S_{j+1}^c$ to a critical ratio $\sigma(.)$ that can be easily tabulated as a function of $j$, $n$, $P_m/P_c$, and $I_j/I_0$. We provide $\sigma(.)$ values specific to our application in Table 3.1. Similar tables can be devised for selling seasons of different length (i.e., $n$), in-season changing sales data availability (i.e., $j$), and other relevant inventory and price ratios (i.e., $I_j/I_0$ and $P_m/P_c$, respectively).

To illustrate how the retailer can make use of the information provided in Table 3.1, let us assume that every week it can choose three possible markdown values. These correspond to the price ratios $P_m/P_c$ of 0.90, 0.75, and 0.50. At the end of week 1, when an inventory ratio $I_j/I_0$ of 0.90 is experienced, no economically viable markdowns can be offered at a price markdown of 25% or 50% off. A markdown of 10% off, however, seems to be appropriate if the sales ratio at the end of week 2, with and without the markdown in place, is expected to exceed the critical value of 1.33. As the retailer does not take a permanent price cut after the first week, it experiences at the end of the second week an inventory ratio $I_j/I_0$ of 0.83. In this case, markdowns valued at 10% or 25% of the initial price seem to be economically viable. To be so, they must lead to

*Table 3.1. Critical Ratio σ(.) for Assessing the Economic Viability of Price Markdowns*

| Inventory ratio $I_j/I_0$ | Week 1 ($j = 1$) Price ratio $P_m/P_c$ | | | Week 2 ($j = 2$) Price ratio $P_m/P_c$ | | |
|---|---|---|---|---|---|---|
| | 0.90 | 0.75 | 0.50 | 0.90 | 0.75 | 0.50 |
| 0.99 | 1.12 | 1.37 | 2.17 | 1.12 | 1.35 | 2.07 |
| 0.98 | 1.13 | 1.41 | 2.41 | 1.12 | 1.36 | 2.15 |
| 0.97 | 1.14 | 1.46 | 2.81 | 1.12 | 1.38 | 2.25 |
| 0.96 | 1.16 | 1.52 | 3.80 | 1.13 | 1.40 | 2.37 |
| 0.95 | 1.17 | 1.61 | | 1.14 | 1.43 | 2.52 |
| 0.94 | 1.19 | 1.73 | | 1.14 | 1.45 | 2.73 |
| 0.93 | 1.22 | 1.91 | | 1.15 | 1.48 | 3.02 |
| 0.92 | 1.25 | 2.29 | | 1.15 | 1.51 | 3.50 |
| 0.91 | 1.28 | | | 1.16 | 1.55 | 4.68 |
| 0.90 | 1.33 | | | 1.17 | 1.59 | |
| 0.89 | 1.39 | | | 1.18 | 1.64 | |
| 0.88 | 1.49 | | | 1.19 | 1.70 | |
| 0.87 | 1.65 | | | 1.20 | 1.77 | |
| 0.86 | 2.16 | | | 1.21 | 1.86 | |
| 0.85 | | | | 1.22 | 1.99 | |
| 0.84 | | | | 1.24 | 2.18 | |
| 0.83 | | | | 1.26 | 2.52 | |
| 0.82 | | | | 1.27 | | |
| 0.81 | | | | 1.30 | | |
| 0.80 | | | | 1.32 | | |

*Note.* n = 16; blank entries refer to cases where an economically viable markdown does not exist.

projected increases in sales at the end of week 3 as reflected by the critical ratios $\sigma(.)$ of 1.26 and 2.52, respectively.

This procedure sheds light on how a retailer could approach the price markdown of its slow-moving items. The underlying concepts can be employed repeatedly to resemble the mechanics of a dynamic process. This means that at the time the first markdown is taken, the entire process is reinitialized to reflect the latest market conditions. Similarly, the implementation of all subsequent markdowns is followed by a mandatory model parameter value reestimation.

## Price Markdowns and Linear Programming

Fashion retailers are often limited by the fashion designers/houses on the timing and range of prices they can charge for the brand name merchandise. To gain more control over their pricing functions, many of these retailers have developed their own private label brands, which are sold exclusively through their network of stores. Macy's, for example, targets customers with various needs through its suite of private brands including

Alfani (men/women), Charter Club (women), Club Room (men), and Greendog (children). Similarly, Saks Fifth Avenue's Men's Collection and Bloomingdale's The Men's Store attempt to appeal to sophisticated yet price-conscious shoppers in need of quality menswear. The trend has been also embraced by online fashion retailers who could not let such an opportunity slip away. The giant ShopBop.com, for example, has introduced its own brand, Bop Basics, as an alternative for its customers to the more expensive designer collections. BlueFly.com has tried to achieve similar goals by introducing and promoting its private label brands including Harrison, Hayden, and Cullen.

From an operations perspective, private labels allow style and seasonal goods retailers to be more responsive to the markets they serve. In particular, since no binding agreements with the design houses are in place to specify tight pricing terms and markdown conditions, fashion retailers can use price as an effective means to drive profitability. In the absence of any contractual obligations, two actions are often employed to immediately impact the retailer's bottom line. First, retailers with private labels are free to set the initial markup as low or as high as they would like as there is nothing in place to enforce it to be within a certain range. Second, retailers can take immediate actions and consider a price markdown the moment sales drop and an item starts to underperform.

Motivated by the specific issues put forth by the management of private label brands, we focus on some of the recent efforts of brick-and-mortar and online retailers that attempt to streamline their fashion related markdown practices. In these instances, retailers intend to exploit the pricing flexibility that comes with the selling of private labels to recommend price markdown strategies that would maximize margins. We illustrate this approach using an example from a major online fashion retailer that offers collections consisting of a mix of designer and private label items.

For one of its private label items, the retailer starts the new season with 500 units in stock. Because the supply of the item comes from overseas, the retailer cannot restock the item during the selling season. A typical season at this retailer lasts about 16 weeks. The item's full selling price is €60, which is anticipated to be offered for at least 1 week. If markdowns are needed, the retailer prefers fixed discrete price discounts that can be easily communicated to its customers. For this reason, price markdowns of 25% and 50% off, corresponding to selling prices of €45 and €30, respectively, are considered. All markdowns are permanent and irreversible. While still in the preseason, the retailer wants to understand what its optimal markdown strategies should be based on various probable full-price weekly sales rates. Among these strategies, selling the item at the full price throughout the season is preferred. If this is not profitable because of lower-than-originally expected sales, the retailer wants to explore alternative strategies that account for seasonality, inventory depletion effects, and special online events such as the timing of e-mail campaigns. Furthermore, once the selling season starts, the retailer wants to have dynamic control over its pricing function to be able to revise or implement price markdowns that reflect updated market conditions.

In a business environment such as this one, product demand is always difficult to predict. In many instances, seasonal products show sales patterns that do not repeat from one season to the next. To complicate things further, within the organization itself, opinions are typically divergent on how products will likely perform in the marketplace. Given the uncertainty that surrounds the demand processes, you may ask how fashion retailers can operationalize their markdown initiatives. Often, although individual product histories cannot be recycled to get relevant product intelligence, histories of groups of similar products can be analyzed to learn the likely demand response of a typical group member. For the specific item introduced earlier, the results of such an undertaking are provided in Table 3.2. To estimate the product group demand models, the product group the item belongs to was identified, all items in this group were selected, and multiplicative models of the types discussed in the previous chapter (i.e., model types B-1 and B-2 in Table 2.9) were explored. The product group identification and the within-group product selection are inexpensive tasks that are typically driven by the product hierarchies in use at the retailer. Finding the preferred model specification(s) is a more involved task that builds on existing theory and requires extensive testing and tweaking.

The demand models depicted in Table 3.2 are exponential models of the B-2 type. We prefer this functional form over its B-1 counterpart because it performs marginally better in regard to the quality of the model fit. Since seasonality within the product group appears weak, we do not consider it explicitly. We also prefer to provide only an excerpt from the full output since the product sales baselines are irrelevant to the subsequent markdown optimization process. In our search for the preferred model specification, we build on previous retail studies and find

*Table 3.2. Product Group Demand Modeling*

| | Reduced model | | | | Full model | | | |
|---|---|---|---|---|---|---|---|---|
| | Estimate | Standard errors | *t value* | *p value* | Estimate | Standard errors | *t value* | *p value* |
| *(Irrelevant output removed due to space constraints)* | | | | | | | | |
| Markdown | 1.83 | 0.24 | 7.5 | 0.00 | 1.56 | 0.24 | 6.6 | 0.00 |
| Multiplier  0% off $\delta_1$ | 1.00 | | | | 1.00 | | | |
| Multiplier 25% off $\delta_2$ | 1.58 | | | | 1.48 | | | |
| Multiplier 50% off $\delta_3$ | 2.49 | | | | 2.18 | | | |
| Periods in between 85% and 90% of the selling season (P1) | −1.10 | 0.21 | −5.2 | 0.00 | −0.90 | 0.21 | −4.4 | 0.00 |
| P1 multiplier $\xi_1$ | 0.33 | | | | 0.41 | | | |
| Periods in between 90% and 95% of the selling season (P2) | −1.77 | 0.21 | −8.4 | 0.00 | −1.53 | 0.21 | −7.4 | 0.00 |
| P2 multiplier $\xi_2$ | 0.17 | | | | 0.22 | | | |
| Periods above 95% of the selling season (P3) | −2.28 | 0.19 | −12.1 | 0.00 | −2.04 | 0.19 | −11. | 0.00 |
| P3 multiplier $\xi_3$ | 0.10 | | | | 0.13 | | | |
| Special events (SE) indicator | - | - | - | - | 0.48 | 0.10 | 4.9 | 0.00 |
| SE multiplier $\varsigma$ | - | | | | 1.61 | | | |

Full Model: Multiplier 25% off *1.48 = exp(0.25 × 1.56)* ; P1 multiplier *0.41 = exp(−0.90)* ; SE multiplier *1.61 = exp(0.48)*
Reduced Model: Multiple R-squared: 0.58; Adjusted R-squared: 0.56
Full Model: Multiple R-squared: 0.62; Adjusted R-squared: 0.60
Built-in function: lm (R base version 2.11.1)

that product group sales are time dependent and explained by markdown values and special online events. In spite of our findings, we choose to show results for two competing models to subsequently illustrate the impact the presence of the special online events has on the expected profitability of recommended markdown policies. Focusing on the parameter estimates of the full model, it is obvious that price markdowns impact sales nonlinearly. This is an intuitive result that confirms to the retailer's expectations. In addition, within the product group, we observe that sales tend to decline toward the end of the items' selling season. The retailer speculates that this behavior is mainly a reflection of the assortment being broken, that is, the on-hand inventory not providing a complete selection of colors and sizes. Although more sophisticated approaches can be employed, we model sales' time dependency and, indirectly, the impact of the inventory level and mix using three time-related variables. As shown in Table 3.2, the corresponding parameter estimates are all statistically significant and quite large in magnitude. For example, all else being equal, the last weeks of the selling season are expected to experience about a tenth of the regular sales (i.e., P3 multiplier equals 0.13). Last but not least, we note that the special online events such as the e-mail campaigns tend to positively impact sales on average by a factor of 1.61.

Although specific to an average group product, the insights gained from the figures of Table 3.2 can be used to initialize the computation of the optimal markdown policies. In the absence of any sales data in the preseason, the retailer could explore the likely product performance using hypothetical weekly sales rates. In season, however, it can decide on the best course of action in regard to the pricing of the item based on actual sales rates and continuously updated product-specific demand multipliers. The differentiation of the latter happens throughout the season when relevant information becomes available. For example, all products in a group may start the season with a special online event demand multiplier of 1.61 but could end the season with such multipliers in the 1.25–2.50 range, based on each product's independent performance. Updating the multipliers typically requires the use of various weighted moving averages of which exponential moving average is the most frequently used. Since illustrating the dynamic character of markdown optimization is beyond the scope of this discussion, we show next how the retailer can structure its preseason markdown initiatives to prepare for more accurate in-season pricing decisions. The same underlying markdown mechanism, however, applies to both of these cases.

As part of how it runs its e-business, the retailer sends out customized newsletters intended to promote new collections, raise awareness for specific brands or item groups, or inform customers of imminent sales opportunities. While the effectiveness of these initiatives largely depends on the content of the actual message, the retailer plans to run recurrent e-mail campaigns directly targeting our item's group a week after products are introduced to the market and every 4 weeks thereafter (i.e., weeks 2, 6, 10, and 14). These campaigns are of the same type as those we used to estimate the group-level demand models shown in Table 3.2. Based on discussions among several buyers at the retailer, a consensus has been reached on the market expectations for this important item. In the absence of any auxiliary activities, there are high hopes that the product will sell at full price at a weekly rate of 25 units. In this context, the initial inventory of 500 units is perceived as sufficient to serve the market requirements with a sufficient amount of leftover to create some end-of-the-season e-store excitement through permanent markdowns. To investigate possible preseason strategies for in-season markdowns, the retailer can use the group-level demand multipliers computed previously to adjust the expected baseline sales of 25 units to account for product life cycle events such as markdowns, time dependency, and special online initiatives. Because after purchasing the items the purchase price becomes a sunk cost, the retailer wishes to maximize revenues from the inventory it starts the season with such that several market constraints are satisfied. In formal terms, the retailer needs to solve the following revenue maximization problem:

$$Max \quad z = \sum_{t=1}^{16}\sum_{i=1}^{3}\left(X_{t,i}\cdot p_i\cdot(D\cdot\delta_i)\cdot\xi_t\cdot\varsigma_t\right)+X_s\cdot s$$

S.T. $\quad \sum_{t=1}^{16}\sum_{i=1}^{3}\left(X_{t,i}\cdot(D\cdot\delta_i)\cdot\xi_t\cdot\varsigma_t\right)+X_s=500 \qquad$ (C1: Inventory constraint)

$\qquad \sum_{i=1}^{3}X_{t,i}\leq 1,\quad \forall t\leq 16 \qquad\qquad\qquad$ (C2: Unique or no-price constraint)

$\qquad X_{1,1}=1 \qquad\qquad\qquad\qquad\qquad\qquad\quad$ (C3: First period full-price constraint)

$\qquad X_{t,1}-X_{t+1,1}\geq 0, \qquad\qquad\quad \forall t\leq 15 \quad$ (C4: Decreasing price constraint 1)

$\qquad X_{t,1}+X_{t,2}-X_{t+1,1}-X_{t+1,2}\geq 0, \quad \forall t\leq 15 \quad$ (C5: Decreasing price constraint 2)

$\qquad \sum_{i=1}^{3}X_{t,i}-\sum_{i=1}^{3}X_{t+1,i}\geq 0, \qquad\quad \forall t\leq 15 \quad$ (C6: Decreasing price constraint 3)

$\qquad$ All $X_{t,i}=0$ or $1$, $X_s\geq 0 \qquad\qquad\qquad$ (C7: Sign and value restrictions), where $X_{t,i}$ are 0/1 decision variables that specify whether or not the discrete price $p_i$ is to be offered in week $t$, $p_i$ is one of the possible prices in the discrete price set $S$ = {€60, €45, €30}, $D$ is the baseline sales of 25 units per week, $\delta_i$ is the demand multiplier corresponding to price $p_i$ (see Table 3.2 for values for $\delta_j$), $\xi_t$ is 1 or $\xi_k$ based on the position of the current week $t$ within the selling season (see Table 3.2 for time brackets and values for $\xi_k$), $\varsigma_t$ is 1 or $\varsigma$ based on whether or not a special online event is scheduled for week $t$ (see Table 3.2 for the value for $\varsigma$), $X_s$ is the inventory left over at the end of the season that needs to be salvaged, and $s$ is the unit salvage value of €10.

Constraints C1–C7 bound the optimal solution and enforce inventory limitations and other operations practices in use at the retailer. Constraint C1 limits the amount of inventory the retailer can sell to the initial value of 500 units. Constraints C2 enforce the use of one of the allowed price points in each of the 16 weeks of the selling horizon. Constraint C3 ensures that the item is offered at full price for at least 1 week. Constraints C4–C6 implement the common retail practice that stipulates that price markdowns are irreversible. Lastly, constraint C7 imposes sign and value restrictions on all decision variables. Figure 3.1 shows the demand values $(D \cdot \delta_j) \cdot \xi_t \cdot \varsigma_t$, which enter both the objective function and the C1 constraint. These values are specific to the full model of Table 3.2. To repeat the task for the reduced model, we simply update the $\delta$ and $\xi$ multipliers appropriately and set $\varsigma$ to 1. The corresponding demand profiles should be smoother than those depicted in Figure 3.1.

For the reduced and full demand models of Table 3.2, the solutions of the price markdown optimization problem are provided in Table 3.3. These results suggest that the demand model specifications that describe the item's market performance better lead to more profitable markdown strategies. In this example, by modeling the impact of the special online events explicitly, the retailer is advised to markdown its full price to €45 in week 7, which follows the anticipated e-mail campaign of week 6. In the absence of this intelligence, the retailer is advised to reduce the price to €45 in week 4 or soon after the first e-mail campaign of week 2.

Just because the retailer possesses this type of information before the season starts does not mean that the retailer should stick to this plan once actual demand for the item starts to become available. In particular, once

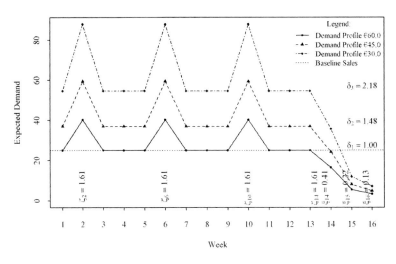

*Figure 3.1. Price-dependent demand profiles.*

*Table 3.3. Preseason Optimal Markdown Policies*

|  | Expected revenue (€) | Markdown policy |
|---|---|---|
| Reduced model | 23,403.1 | Sell at €60.0 for 3 weeks. Switch to €45.0 in week 4. Sell at €45.0 until the end of the season. |
| Full model | 25,156.1 | Sell at €60.0 for 6 weeks. Switch to €45.0 in week 7. Sell at €45.0 until the end of the season. |

R base version 2.11.1
R function: Rglpk_solve_LP (R contributed package: Rglpk version 0.3-5 with the GLPK callable library version 4.42)

the season starts, the retailer should confirm the hypothetical baseline sales used in the preseason markdown optimization exercise. The actual sales, once available, could be used then to rerun the optimization procedure and adjust the depth and the timing of the suggested markdowns. In addition, all product group demand multipliers can be revised in season to reflect the item's actual performance. By dynamically resolving the markdown optimization with updated information, revenues can be maximized and end-of-the-season spoilage can be minimized.

## Chapter Summary

Dynamic pricing is the practice of continuously adjusting prices to maximize profit by shaping demand (through price changes) to meet the available supply. In this chapter, we provide an understanding of how dynamic pricing has evolved and crossed out of the traditional travel and hospitality industry boundaries to become the *new thing* in nontraditional industries such as retailing, utilities, sports events, and the arts. One of the reasons for its increased adoption is the fact that it is now often technologically feasible for each customer to be quoted her own price. We also discuss some contextual factors and subjective situations that impede organizations from employing dynamic pricing successfully.

In light of the trends that have reshaped the style and seasonal goods retailing, we offer some perspectives on why permanent price markdowns—a particular form of dynamic pricing—are used so frequently. While their primary role involves permanent reductions in price in order to clear excess inventory off the sales floor, price markdowns are also sometimes used as demand learning or segmentation mechanisms. Oftentimes, however, the clearing of excess inventory in the absence of any other considerations can be detrimental to an organization. Thus we discuss a relatively newer trend of creating optimal price markdown policies with the explicit goal of maximizing gross margins.

We conclude the chapter with two case studies that illustrate how price markdowns are often dealt with in practice. In the first case study, we show how organizations can identify profitable markdown opportunities for their slow-moving items. In the second, we highlight how organizations can rely on more sophisticated techniques to optimize their markdown policies such that revenues/profits are maximized.

# CHAPTER 4

# Pricing in Business-to-Business Environments

In contrast to the pricing decisions discussed in the first three chapters, which involve estimating a price-quantity relationship, business-to-business (B2B) environments often involve a single bid opportunity where the entire bid amount is either won or lost. The probability that a bid will win is based on, among other things, a price that is customized by the sales organization for that particular customer or bid opportunity. In business environments companies are often required to respond to a potential client's requests-for-proposals (RFPs) with a personalized offer. The customized response to these RFPs reflects the unique customer-company trade conditions and is frequently accompanied by customer-tailored prices that try to balance decreasing margins with increasing bid success probabilities. While customized pricing has always been a common practice in such environments, the actual task of determining the customized price has historically been based purely on the experience and judgment of the salesperson responsible for the customer's account.

More recently, analytical models for customized pricing have been successfully implemented in industries as diverse as package delivery, building products distribution, and hotel event space.[1] The models have also been used in the business-to-consumer (B2C) market in the financial services industry to help banks determine what interest rate to offer when responding to requests for mortgages, credit cards, and car loans.[2] The financial improvement from using customized pricing models can be significant. UPS reported an increase in profits of more than $100 million per year by optimizing its price offerings using customized pricing models.[3]

In a typical B2B environment, price optimization relies on models that incorporate insights gained from the bidding history into the current pricing decisions. Specifically, by using the information on past wins and losses, models are estimated to express the probability of winning the bid as a function of the offered price. These probability curves are commonly termed *bid-response functions*. The two bid-response probability functions previously discussed in chapter 3 are the logit and power models.[4] Both are inverse S-shaped and approach one and zero at low and high prices, respectively. If all firms were homogeneous in their probability of accepting a bid for a given price, the bid-response functions would be the same for all potential firms and the result of the price optimization would be a single price quoted for every bid opportunity.

In practice, however, firms are often heterogeneous in their price sensitivity as predicted by certain customer attributes such as size, location, or the length of time a customer has had a relationship with the bidding firm. Not surprisingly, determining which of the many possible customer attributes are good predictors of a potential firm's price sensitivity is often a difficult task for a salesperson who may respond to hundreds or even thousands of RFPs per year. Thus the fact that bid-response functions can include, and in some cases test the significance of, these different customer attributes makes them attractive tools for firms that desire a more standardized (and analytical) approach to B2B pricing. More specifically, bid-response functions use customers' attribute data along with the firm's historical win/loss data from past bid opportunities to test which attributes are most useful in segmenting customers. Furthermore, they also support the analytical optimization of the price for future bid opportunities based on the significant segmentation groups that were determined using the model-fitting procedures.

Price segments are defined as sets of transactions, classified by customer, product, and transaction attributes, which exhibit similar price sensitivities. Customer attributes may include customer location, size of the market the customer is in, type of business the customer is in, the way the customer uses the product, customer purchase frequency, customer size, and customer purchasing sophistication. Product attributes may include product type, life-cycle stage, and the degree of commoditization. Transaction attributes may include order size, other products on the order, channel (the potential buyer is reached through), specific competitors, when the order is placed, and the urgency of the bidder. In addition, some models assume knowledge of the historical and current bid price of competing firms participating in the bid opportunity.

A common characteristic of environments where firms employ customized pricing models occurs when the bidder with the lowest price does not always win the bid. Thus markets are characterized by product differentiation where a given firm may command a positive price premium over its competitors, dependent on the particular customer requesting the bid response. Sometimes even bids from the same customer may contain some inherent amount of uncertainty in the bid-winning probability because the bid-requesting firm randomly allocates its business to different competitors to ensure a competitive market for future bids. Because of these practices, a firm will never be able to remove all uncertainty from the bid-price response process and must work with probabilistic models.

A second common characteristic of an appropriate environment occurs when the size of the bid opportunities is not large enough to justify a sales person dedicated to each customer. Instead, a single sales person may respond to multiple bid opportunities from a variety of potential customers each day. The most common alternatives to using customized pricing models are either to charge a fixed price to all customers or to have a sales agent respond to each separate bid opportunity with a customized price. Charging a fixed price leads to missed opportunities to price discriminate among different customer segments—a practice that has been well publicized for significantly increasing a firm's profit in many different industries. The other alternative, relying on a sales agent to respond to multiple bid opportunities, is also problematic. Theoretically, the sales agent should have knowledge of the market, based on the customer's history of former bid responses, allowing the sales agent to customize a price that optimizes this inherent trade-off between decreasing margins, due to lowering the price, and increasing probabilities of winning the bid. In reality, sales agents often do not make good trade-off decisions in these situations because of either a lack of historical knowledge, the inability to process this historical knowledge into probability distributions, or misaligned incentives.[5] The judicious use of customized pricing models allows firms to capture historical bid information, analyze it, and present nonbiased price recommendations for future bidding opportunities. If there is additional information available regarding the bidding opportunity that cannot be captured in the model, the model's recommended price may serve as one of many possible inputs to the person responsible for making the bid-response decision. Additional background and information on where customized pricing models are best applied can be found in Phillips.[6]

## Relation to Traditional Price Optimization

The practice of price optimization is well known for applications where the demand for a product over a certain period of time is correlated with the price charged for the product over the same time period. In such a situation, a firm can measure the demand at different price points for a product and use this data to estimate a price-response function. This traditional application to price optimization works well in environments where there are a large number of potential customers who each may buy a small quantity of the product (e.g., consumer retail stores) or where a small number of potential customers purchase large quantities of a product but spread their purchases over many suppliers (e.g., commodity spot markets such as grain, steel, or oil). It is less helpful, however, in winner-take-all bidding situations that are common in B2B transactions, where the customer commits to purchase a given quantity of goods or services and solicits bids from a set of firms capable of providing that quantity. In these situations, the decision a providing firm is concerned about is not if (or how much) the customer will buy but rather will the customer buy from the firm as opposed to one of its competitors. Thus the provider firm does not face a decision of what price to place on a product to attract demand but instead what price to quote to this particular customer to win this particular bid opportunity (customized pricing).

Figure 4.1 shows a historical demand plot for a customized pricing scenario. Notice that the wins (indicated by values of one) are more common for the lower prices while the losses (indicated by values of zero) are more common for the higher prices.

The data captured in Figure 4.1 is the historical win/loss data for a firm over 150 past bid opportunities for the same product. Judging from the data, it appears that the average price offered has been around $10 per unit but the firm has historically priced as low as $8 and as high as a little over $12. It also appears that a lower-than-average price does

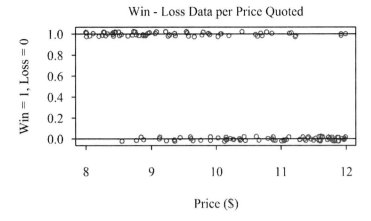

*Figure 4.1. Historical demand data for customized pricing.*

not guarantee a win, nor does a higher-than-average price guarantee a loss—there is some uncertainty in the demand. Therefore, we will focus on maximizing the firm's expected profit, consisting of the total profit assuming the firm wins the bid (margin multiplied by the quantity, Q) times the probability of winning a bid for a given price, which we label $\rho(P) \in [0,1]$. Thus the firm's expected profit is $\pi(P) = (P - C) \cdot Q \cdot \rho(P)$.

## Estimating the Probability Function

Once $\rho(P)$ is estimated, the actual price optimization part for the problem is straightforward and differs little from the traditional linear demand problem. The difficulty, of course, lies in estimating $\rho(P)$. Before we discuss some various methods of doing so, it is helpful to define some properties that any estimated function should possess. First, the function should decrease monotonically as the price increases. Second, the function should be bounded by zero and one (Figure 4.2).

While there are several models that provide a reverse S-shaped probability function, the most common model used in practice is the logit model, a model similar in spirit to the one described in the first two chapters. This model is described in Boyd et al. and Phillips and is compared against a competing model in Agrawal and Ferguson.[7] As a review, the logit model is represented by

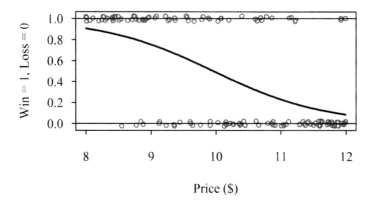

**Figure 4.2. Fitted reverse S-shaped probability function to win/loss data.**

$$\rho(P) = \frac{C \cdot e^{a+b \cdot P}}{1 + e^{a+b \cdot P}}, \qquad (4.1)$$

where $C = 1$ and $a$ and $b$ are parameters that must be estimated to fit the historical win/loss data. The parameter estimation is performed by minimizing the squared errors of the residuals or by using maximum-likelihood estimates. Before estimating the parameter values of the models, however, it is important to divide the historical win/loss dataset into two segments, one for estimating the parameter values and the other for measuring the fit. Similar to time series–forecasting models, measuring the goodness-of-fit on the same data as the parameter values may result in a misleadingly close fit as compared to testing the model on a holdout sample. Phillips describes how each estimation method is applied to the logit function.[8] In general, if we define each historical bid opportunity with the subscript $i$ (with $W_i$ representing the indicator response variable, $1 = $ win and $0 = $ loss, and $P_i$ representing the firm's price response for bid opportunity $i$), the most common estimation method is to choose parameter values $(a, b)$ that maximize the likelihood of the observed values:

$$Max \prod_i \left( \rho\left(P_i \mid a, b\right)^{W_i} \cdot \left(1 - \rho(P_i \mid a, b)\right)^{(1-W_i)} \right) \qquad (4.2)$$

### Price Optimization for Customized Pricing

We now look at how customized pricing probability models are used in price optimization. For the following discussion, our objective is to maximize expected profits. However, other strategic or operational objectives can be easily accommodated such as increasing market share or including constraints on capacity, inventory, price, or margin. In addition, the firm is assumed to be risk-neutral in this example. A risk-averse firm may prefer to optimize expected revenue with a concave utility function so as to mitigate the chances of bad individual outcomes. The price optimization problem for bid opportunity $i$ (with $Q_i$ now representing the quantity that is requested in bid $i$) is

$$\underset{P_i}{Max}\ \pi\left(P_i\right) = \rho\left(P_i\right) \cdot \left(P_i - C\right) \cdot Q_i. \tag{4.3}$$

Note that the margin $(P_i - C)$ is strictly increasing in price (see panel A in Figure 4.3) but the probability of winning the bid is strictly decreasing in price (see panel B in Figure 4.3). Therefore, the expected profit is often a unimodal function as shown in Figure 4.4.

Determining the optimal price involves finding a global maximum for the expected profit. Since the profit function is unimodal, any search-based optimization algorithm can be used to solve for the price that maximizes profit, including the solver package available in Microsoft

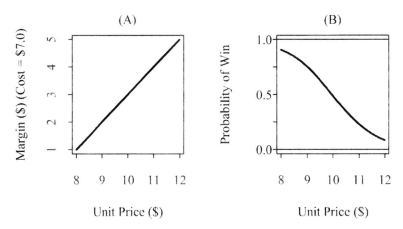

Figure 4.3. (A) Marginal deal contribution versus unit price, (B) probability of win versus unit price.

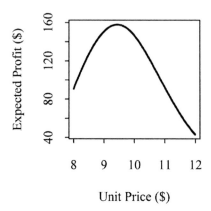

**Figure 4.4. Expected profit versus unit price.**

Excel. The profit-maximizing price can also be found by solving for the price where the elasticity of the expected profit function is equal to the inverse of the marginal contribution ratio.

## Segmenting Customers Based on Historical Price Behavior

The basic logit model described in equation (4.1) only includes the price as a predictor of the probability of winning a bid. This model is appropriate if there are no discernable differences in the price sensitivity of a firm's customer set; every customer has the same probability, for every bid opportunity, of accepting the firm's bid at a given price. In this situation, the customized price optimization equation (4.2) will recommend the same optimal price for every future bid opportunity. In practice, this is rarely the case—if it was, then why would the firm be applying customized pricing to begin with? A more common scenario is one where a firm's sales force has historically set different prices for each bid opportunity based on certain characteristics of the bid or of the customer requesting the bid. The characteristics driving the different prices, which may even differ by salespersons within a firm, may include such things as the size of the customer (annual revenue), the length of time a firm has been a customer, the quantity requested by the bid, or the number of firms offered to submit to this particular bidding opportunity. Thus a bid opportunity from a small customer who has had a long-term relationship with the firm and typically involves only two additional firms in the bidding process may receive a higher price quote than a large customer with little sales history who includes at least five competitive quotes in every bid opportunity. In an interesting example of customized pricing in the banking industry, Kadet describes how some banks place consumers into pricing segments and quote customized interest rates each time a potential customer shops for a loan.[9] It is exactly this case, when customers can be segmented based on their price sensitivities, that customized pricing models provide the largest benefit.

The logit model equation (4.1) can be expanded to include segmentation variables. To show how, we use an example from an application of customized pricing at a major credit bureau, which is a real company that we will call Alpha Company because of the sensitive nature of the dataset. Alpha sells credit scores of individuals to businesses that extend credit to their customers, such as car dealerships and jewelry stores. If an individual purchases her or her credit score, there is a list price of around $10. Businesses that purchase multiple credit scores annually often send out bids to the three largest credit bureaus, promising a minimum volume of score requests per year in exchange for a discounted price. Alpha is typically included in these bid opportunities, so it has a substantial historical database that includes each past bid opportunity, the size of the minimum quantity promised in each contract, and the length of time in months that the business requesting the bid has been a customer of Alpha. We denote the quantity of each bid by $Q$ and the length of the relationship with Alpha in months by $M$. In addition, we define $c$ as the coefficient for the quantity parameter and $d$ as the coefficient for the length of the relationship. Including these new variables and coefficients into equation (4.1) results in

$$\rho(P|Q,M) = \frac{e^{a+b\cdot P+c\cdot Q+d\cdot M}}{1+e^{a+b\cdot P+c\cdot Q+d\cdot M}}. \tag{4.4}$$

The estimation of the coefficients ($a$, $b$, $c$, $d$) is performed through a maximum likelihood fit. It still remains, however, to determine what segmentation variables should be included in the model. Just because a firm has historical data for a segmentation variable does not mean that it should be included in the model. Next, we will explain how to determine whether a segmentation variable should be included.

Many different approaches to segment data exist. The number and type of segments can be determined in advance (a priori), such as asking the sales team what customer characteristics they use when determining the price to respond to a bid. While this knowledge (perhaps based on years of experience) should not be discounted, it should, however, be statistically tested. There are many cases where a firm implementing a customized pricing model finds, when doing so, that many of the characteristics it has historically used to segment customers are not statistically significant based on the historical sales data. Thus it is also useful to determine (or confirm) customer segments based on data analyses (post hoc). Some methods for determining customer segments include nonoverlapping and overlapping clustering methods, classification and regression trees, and Expectation Maximization algorithms. A detailed analysis of these methods is beyond the scope of this chapter, but we refer the reader to Wedel and Kamakura for a detailed overview.[10] In most situations, the easiest and most popular method, however, is to run a logistic regression.[11] This technique is available in most statistical software packages and, similar to linear regression, a statistical significance test can be applied to the predictor variables. Estimating the win/loss probability as a function of price, quantity and active months by running a logistic regression on Alpha's data results in the output shown in Table 4.1.

**Table 4.1. Output From Logistic Regression on Alpha's Historical Win/Loss Data**

| Variable | Estimate | p value |
|---|---|---|
| Constant | –0.27 | 0.05 |
| Quantity | 0.00 | 0.66 |
| Price | –0.23 | 0.01 |
| Active months | 0.36 | 0.00 |

Observing the *p values* in the regression output table shows that only the constant, the price, and the active months are significant at the 95% level (*p value* less than 0.05). Thus the quantity variable is dropped from the model, and a second regression is run using only the significant variables. The estimated coefficients of the variables from the second regression are shown in Table 4.2.

**Table 4.2. Output From Logistic Regression After Removing Quantity**

| Variable | Estimate | *p value* |
|---|---|---|
| Constant | −0.21 | 0.04 |
| Price | −0.24 | 0.00 |
| Active months | 0.36 | 0.00 |

Substituting the estimated coefficient values into equation (4.3) leaves

$$p\left(P|M\right) = \frac{e^{-0.21-0.24\cdot P+0.36\cdot M}}{1+e^{-0.21-0.24\cdot P+0.36\cdot M}}. \tag{4.5}$$

The fact that quantity was not a significant segmentation variable was a surprise to the sales team at Alpha. Prior to this study, the team members felt that the quantity requested in a bid was a better indicator of the price sensitivity of the customer than the length of time the customer had been doing business with Alpha. Of course, there may be other significant segmentation variables that were not included in the model, such as geographic location, company size, and so on. Moving forward, Alpha plans on collecting additional information on each bidding opportunity so that other possible segmentation variables can be tested. In general, the number of customer attributes (segments) that can be accurately estimated depends on the amount of historical bid information available. If extensive historical data are available, greater degrees of segmentation can be achieved without compromising the accuracy and robustness of the statistical estimation of the parameter values.

While building statistically significant probability models is important, what firms really care about are improvements in profits. In the next section, we show how to test the performance of a customized pricing model.

## Measuring Performance

We alluded to the point earlier that the historical win/loss data should be divided into an estimation set and a holdout sample set. A holdout set is critical for obtaining a realistic measure of the model's performance; it is misleading to measure performance on the same data that was used to estimate the model's coefficients. There are two performance metrics available: percent improvement in profits over unoptimized actual profits and percent improvement in profits over unoptimized expected profits. To understand the difference between the two performance metrics, consider the following bid opportunity from Alpha's historical win/loss data:

| | |
|---|---|
| Bid identifier | 451 |
| Win | Yes |
| Order size | 240 |
| Active months | 0 |
| Original bid price | $3.92 |
| Optimal bid price | $5.15 |
| Win probability at original bid price | 0.24 |
| Win probability at optimized bid price | 0.19 |

Applying the logit model from equation (4.4) to the bid opportunity and optimizing results in an optimal price of $5.15 for this particular bid opportunity. Substituting in the original bid price of $3.92 into equation (4.4) results in the probability of winning for the unoptimized bid of 0.24 or 24%. Substituting the optimal price results in a probability of winning for the optimized bid of 0.19 or 19%.

Since Alpha's marginal cost of providing a credit score is essentially zero, the actual profit from this bid opportunity is (Original Unit Price – Marginal Cost) · Order Size · Win/Loss Indicator Variable = $(3.92 – 0) · 240 · 1 = $940.80. If the original bid had resulted in a loss, the actual profit would be zero. The original bid expected profit is (Original Unit Price – Marginal Cost) · Order Size · Win Probability at the Original Bid Price = $(3.92 – 0) · 240 · 0.24 = $225.79. Note that the expected profit is always smaller than the actual profit when the bid was won, and is always larger when the bid was lost. The optimized bid expected profit is (Optimized Price – Marginal Cost) · Order Size · Win Probability at the Optimized Bid Price = $(5.15-0) · 240 · 0.19 = $235.60. These figures can then be used to calculate the two performance measure for this bid opportunity as follows:

Percent improvement in optimized bid expected
profits over unoptimized bid actual profits =
($235.60 – $940.80)/$940.80 = –0.75 = –75%

and

Percent improvement in optimized bid expected
profits over unoptimized bid expected profits =
($235.60 – $225.79)/$225.79 = 0.04 = 4%.

These calculations should be performed for every bid opportunity in the holdout set and the sum of each measure (over each bid opportunity in the holdout set) can then be used as a measure of performance for the model. For this dataset (holdout sample equal to 160 historical bids), the total percent improvement in actual profits was 137% and the total percent improvement in expected profits was 112%.

## Implementing a Customized Pricing Optimization Package

Thus far, we have focused on the technical aspects of customized pricing optimization. What is clearly evident, however, from the presentations by individuals whose firms have implemented customized pricing models is that the most difficult part of an implementation is not the proof of the value of the system, nor is it building the models and performing the price optimizations. Instead, the most quoted difficulty involves the acceptance of the system's price recommendations by the existing sales team. The removal of some decision-making authority away from individuals to a more automated system is problematic in any environment, but it is particularly difficult for pricing, since the sales team may feel that the ability to generate customized price quotes is a large part of the value its members bring to the firm and the incentive system (often a commission based on total revenue) may not match the profit maximization objective of a customized pricing optimization system.

Are there best practices that may be applied to help mitigate these problems given the almost certain cultural issues and expected resistance to a system implementation? It turns out that there are some practices that seem to help, based on the same panel discussions referenced earlier. The most frequently suggested technique is to treat the customized price optimizer as a decision support tool for the sales team rather than a system that will automatically set prices for all future bid opportunities. No automated pricing system will ever completely replace the ability of humans to factor in extenuating circumstances or information that is not captured in the historical sales data. Of course, sales personnel often overemphasize the value of human judgment so there needs to be some incentive to follow the recommendations of the pricing models. One such incentive that has worked for several firms is to track the frequency that a sales person sets a price within the recommended range from the pricing model and then publish these results along with the monthly profits made by each sales person. If, as expected, the sales personnel ranked the highest for pricing within the recommended price ranges are also ranked the highest for monthly profits, then the rest of the sales team will copy this practice to improve their own performance.

## Chapter Summary

To summarize, the following steps are involved in building a customized pricing optimization model:

1. Start with a historical dataset of the firm's previous bid opportunities for the product of interest. This dataset should include both wins and losses along with the price submitted for each bid opportunity and any other segmentation data available on the customer or bid. The historical dataset should be randomly divided into two distinct sets: the first for estimating the model parameter values and the second for performance evaluation (the holdout data).

2. A win/loss probability model, such as the logit model, should be developed that includes coefficients for any segmentation variables.

3. Using the estimation set from the historical data, the parameter values for the probability model should be estimated using maximum likelihood estimators. This can be done by running a logistic regression if a logit model is used for the probability model. The output from the regression will identify the segmentation variables that are significant.

4. After selecting the win/loss probability model that provides the best fit for the holdout sample data, use this model to optimize the bid prices for all the bids in the holdout set from the historic data.

5. Percent improvements over expected profits and over actual profits can then be calculated using the holdout data to measure the model's performance.

While customized pricing models hold great potential for substantially increasing profits, any firm considering adopting price models for customized pricing needs to be aware of their limitations. The models behind customized pricing assume the bid opportunities are exogenous and are not affected by the bid responses suggested through the optimization. In reality, a firm's pricing strategy may have a significant impact on customer retention, especially if the optimization model recommends consistently pricing higher than the competition for a particular customer class. Also, the optimization models do not assume any strategic response from the firm's competitors. Instead, they assume the actions of competitors will stay the same as it was during the time period covered by the historical dataset. In reality, competitors may react to a firm's new pricing strategy causing the historical bid opportunity data to be unrepresentative of future bid price responses. To help detect these possibilities, mechanisms should be put in place to monitor and evaluate the performance of the models over time. If competitors change their bid-pricing behavior due to the implementation of a customized pricing solution, more involved models using concepts from game theory should be employed.

# CHAPTER 5

# Customer Behavior Aspects of Pricing

Thus far, we have mainly focused on observing how customers respond to different prices and then using this data to estimate models so that price can be optimized. A purely analytical approach to price optimization does not guarantee success, however. What is also needed is to understand why customers react the way they do to promotions and price changes so the changes and promotions can be framed in a way that maximizes customer acceptance. To do so, we now venture into the psychology of pricing.

Before getting into specifics, let us first try a simple mental exercise. Imagine that you are trying out a new restaurant for dinner with a friend or significant other. You decide that a Merlot will provide a nice pairing with your meal choice so you ask for the wine menu. The waiter then hands you a wine menu that has the following two options for Merlot wines:

| | |
|---|---|
| Dan River Vineyards Merlot | $25 |
| Dan River Vineyards Merlot Reserve | $35 |

Which bottle do you choose? Let's repeat the exact same exercise with the only difference being that, when you open the wine menu, you observe the following options for Merlot wines:

| | |
|---|---|
| Dan River Vineyards Merlot | $25 |
| Dan River Vineyards Merlot Reserve | $35 |
| Dan River Vineyards Merlot Limited | $45 |

Now, which bottle did you choose? It is doubtful that you recognize the brand of the wine (in fact, it is a made up name), so you cannot rely on past experience of the brand's quality to aid in your selection. In similar experiments of settings such as this, the majority of customers faced with the $25 and $35 bottles of wine have chosen the $25 bottle. The main reason provided after the choice is made is that they do not recognize the brand so they chose the least expensive option so as to limit their risk if the wine is not good. What is interesting is that the majority of customers provided with the three different wine choices (the $25, $35, and $45 bottles) have chosen the $35 bottle.

If the restaurant follows the common convention of increasing the markups with the cost of the product, then it is reasonable to assume that the $35 bottle provides around $15 in profit, while the $25 bottle provides around $10. If we also assume the common convention that the restaurant basically breaks even on sales of its meals and makes all its profit from the sale of beverages, then the restaurant could increase its per-seating profit by 33% simply by adding the third wine bottle option to their menu.

While this example is intentionally oversimplified, it demonstrates a commonly observed phenomenon in pricing-related experiments that cannot be explained by the microeconomics-based theory of pricing that was discussed in chapter 1. If we assume away budget constraints, basic microeconomic theory states that each customer derives a distinct utility from every possible product. In this context, the customer chooses to purchase if the product utility (expressed as a monetary value) is greater than the selling price and selects the product that maximizes her remaining utility. There is nothing in microeconomic "utility" theory that explains why a customer would change her decision from purchasing the $25 bottle to purchasing the $35 bottle simply because a third option (the $45 bottle) was added to the menu. To better understand this decision making, we have to venture into the psychological aspects of pricing and to something called a reference price.

## Reference Pricing

The wine selection experiment is an example of reference pricing, sometimes called anchoring. In the wine example, the consumers' price sensitivity appears to change simply by changing the assortment of products that are available. In other experiments, their price sensitivity changes based on the order that an offer is presented. For example, an oceanfront hotel at a popular tourist destination ran an experiment in which half of its reservation center operators presented the most expensive room in the hotel first (oceanfront room), then offered the less expensive room (parking lot–view room) while emphasizing the discount from the more expensive option. The other half of the operators presented the room options in the opposite order. After running the experiment for several days, the reservation operators who presented the more expensive room first had a significantly higher percentage of customers who booked a room, as well as significantly higher total revenue from the bookings they accepted.

Another aspect of reference pricing describes how a buyer's price sensitivity increases with a higher price compared to perceived alternatives. The key word in this definition is perceived. As an example, during the recession in the travel and hospitality industry in the early 2000s, many hotel chains dramatically lowered their room rates in order to keep occupancy levels at a reasonable level. Thus a hotel that normally charged $300 per night would lower the rack rate to $150 per night. After the economy started to recover, the hotel chains tried to raise their rack rates back to their original amounts. Doing so, however, initially resulted in significant decreases in demand—much below the baseline demand that occurred for the same room rates before the recession, even though the overall economy had returned to its prerecession levels. A generally accepted reason within the industry for this increase in price sensitivity was that customers had formed new reference prices for the value of the hotel rooms. Thus if a customer began to value a particular hotel room at $150, then an increase in the price to $300 is perceived to be unfair. The hotel chains learned from this experience, however. When the next recession occurred in the latter 2000s, the hotel chains were very careful about lowering the actual room rates to stimulate demand. Instead, they offered deals such as the fourth night free or free breakfasts with a room stay. These offers often accomplished the same result of stimulating additional demand but without the negative effect of changing the perceived reference prices of their customers for the value of a hotel stay.

Retailers also have to be aware of changing their customers' reference price for an item during promotions or when practicing dynamic pricing. If the price for an item is lowered for too long of a time period, customers will change the perceived value they associate with the product and will be reluctant to purchase the product again at the former baseline price. Thus sales should be announced and the time period should be set for reasonably short duration.

It should also be noted in this discussion that certain items can form a reference price for an entire store. Consumers are more aware of the "market" price of some items more than others. For grocery stores, an item that consumers frequently use to determine the price competitiveness of a store is the price for a gallon of milk. Since most consumers buy milk every week, they tend to be very aware of its price. Thus if they enter a particular store for the first time and notice that the store prices a gallon of milk significantly higher than what they are used to paying (above their reference price), they will form an impression of the entire store as being a high-cost location. If, by comparison, the store prices an item such as nail clippers significantly higher than its competitors, consumers may not even notice this price difference since they tend to buy nail clippers infrequently. For this reason, the price range for a gallon of milk is fairly small among competing stores, while the price range for items bought less frequently may exhibit a wide range of prices. One of the hottest topics in retailing is the science of determining which items and categories consumers have a more knowledgeable understanding of market prices for.

A final topic on reference pricing is how market prices, or some surrogate of them, are increasingly used in the pricing analytics models employed by some of the pricing software firms. As an example, a major hotel chain implemented a price optimization software that uses, as a reference price in the model, the average daily room rate of a hotel's closest five competitors. For example, a hotel property in a downtown location that caters mostly to business clients uses, as a reference price, the average daily room rate of five competing hotel properties near the same downtown location. You may wonder how the hotel collects the prices from the competitive hotels daily. Since most rates in the hospitality industry are published on the Internet, there are several companies that specialize in designing web bots, programs that automatically capture the prices quoted on other firms' web pages. These professional "screen-scraping" firms assemble a vast database of rates for each hotel property, by date and by room type, and send updated reports, listing the rates of a set number of their competitors, daily. These competitor prices are then fed into a firm's pricing optimization software where they often form the basis for a reference price.

There is still a lot that is unknown about how consumers develop their reference prices. To illustrate just how arbitrary reference pricing can be, Dan Ariely (a professor at MIT and now Duke University) ran a series of behavioral experiments to see how memory of an unrelated set of numbers influenced how consumers bid for items. Ariely and his coauthors chose items such as an unknown brand of wine, cordless keyboards, and Belgian chocolates, because they represent items that most people have no strong priors for prices. They began the experiment by asking the participants (in this case, MIT students) to write the last two digits of their Social Security numbers on a sheet of paper. The participants were then divided into five groups based on a ranked order of these two digits (00–19, 20–39, etc.). Each subgroup was presented with the same items and asked to provide a bid for each item. While one would expect that five random groups (the last two numbers of each participant's Social Security number should be random) have the same average bids, the average bids showed a consistent positive correlation with the last two Social Security numbers. That is, the bids from the group that wrote down the last two numbers of 00–19 bid consistently lower for all the items than did the group with the last two numbers 80–99.

The main implication of reference prices to pricing decisions is that when a firm decides to offer a temporary price promotion, care must be taken to ensure that the promotional price does not change the consumers' reference price for the product. While reference prices have a significant impact on how consumers respond to price changes, exactly how they respond depends on whether the observed price is higher or lower than the reference price. Their response also depends on how much higher or lower the price is. This leads to our next discussion on prospect theory.

## Prospect Theory

Prospect theory describes a behavioral approach to human decision making developed by Daniel Kahneman and Amos Tversky in 1979 to help explain deviations from economic models of rationality.[1] Most of their results relate to the treatment of uncertainty and are not directly relevant to pricing, but one specific finding has important implications for pricing: the asymmetric, and nonlinear, treatment of how people view gains and losses.

To explain, let's try another thought experiment. Imagine that you put on a coat that you had not worn for a while and found a $5 bill in the pocket that you did not know that you had. This experience will typically raise your happiness level by a certain amount. Now imagine that you just realized that you mistakenly left a $5 bill on a table in the library, and it is not there when you return. This experience will typically lower your level of happiness. One of the interesting findings from prospect theory is that the loss of the money lowers your happiness more than you gain in happiness from finding the money. Thus changes in utility are asymmetric between gains and losses—losses are experienced more intensely than gains.

Another important finding is that there is a nonlinear and decreasing return to gains. Think of the coat example again, but imagine that you found $10 in the pocket rather than $5. Finding the $5 increased your state of happiness by 20%, but finding $10 will not necessarily increase your state of happiness by 40%, or twice the amount that finding the $5 did. Thus increases in our gains result in an increase in our utility, but there are diminishing returns. There is a similar relationship with losses. Discovering that you left $10 on the table instead of $5 does not necessarily mean that you will be twice as upset.

The graph in Figure 5.1 illustrates both aspects of prospect theory. The loss in value from the 10% loss is greater than the gain in value from the 10% gain. The graph also illustrates the nonlinear relationship for both gains and losses. Extending prospect theory to pricing results in two general rules of thumb: (a) offer a discount rather than charge a premium whenever possible, and (b) small discounts have disproportionate effects, larger discounts proportionately less effect. The first rule reflects the asymmetry between gains and losses. Consumers view price increases or surcharges as a loss and view price discounts or promotions as a gain. Thus it is better to start with a higher base price and offer discounts than start with a lower base price and charge surcharges. The second rule implies that firms can delight their customers with even small discounts, but they should expect diminishing returns from the value their customers perceive as the discount increases. Note that this relationship is different from the shape of the price-response functions that we discussed in chapters 1 and 2 (i.e., prospect theory does not discredit the use of a linear demand curve, for example). Prospect theory pertains to how an individual customer's utility changes with a gain or loss, while the price-response curves reflect how the total market will react to price changes.

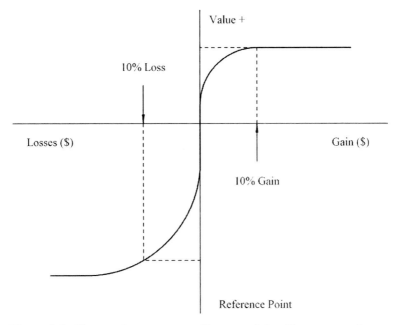

*Figure 5.1. Changes in consumer utility as explained by prospect theory.*

The main implications of prospect theory for pricing decisions are that discounts are more acceptable than surcharges, and small discounts can often capture a large percentage of the benefit of large discounts. Thus far, we have focused on how some behavioral aspects affect whether consumers decide to make a purchase or not. We have yet to say much about how consumers feel after making a purchase, that is, customer satisfaction. In the next section, we address this important topic with a discussion on perceived fairness.

## Perceived Fairness of Pricing

Have you ever purchased an item, feeling pleased with the transaction, only to discover a short time period later that the same item has been marked down or that someone you know purchased the same item for a much lower price? If so, how did you feel about your purchase after this new revelation? If you are like most people, your satisfaction from making the purchase will change from positive to negative. The first example is termed *buyer regret*, while the second example is termed *interpersonal comparisons*, because it often results when two customers of the same product discuss their purchase transaction and one person discovers that the other person paid a lower price.

Some industries are more susceptible to the influence of interpersonal comparisons than others. For example, it is common for airlines or hotels to charge very different prices to customers for the same flight or the same room on the same date at the same hotel. Consumers in these industries rarely interact with each other, so they suffer from a minimum amount of loss of customer satisfaction from these practices. The cruise line industry, by comparison, groups their customers together for social events and meals during a multiday cruise, where the topic of conversation frequently turns to what each party paid for their cruise. Thus the cruise line industry must be diligent about managing interpersonal comparisons, lest its customers leave the cruise with a diminished satisfaction level.

Firms also have to be aware of how price changes are perceived by consumers. In general, most consumers believe that they are entitled to a reasonable price and that firms are entitled to a reasonable profit. They also feel that it is unfair for a firm to make what are perceived to be abnormally high profits, even when customers are willing to buy the product at a high price. Examples of this principle abound, whenever there is a systematic shortage of a hot-selling product or when there is a demand/supply imbalance due to things such as natural disasters. This idea, called dual entitlement, was presented by Kahneman, Knetsch, and Thaler.[2] The implications of this principle for pricing decisions are as follows: (a) raising price to recoup costs is usually viewed as fair, while raising prices just to increase profits is often viewed as unfair, and (b) it generally helps to provide reasons when implementing price increases.

Finally, consumers tend to view differentiable pricing between customers more favorably when they feel that the lower price is at least theoretically achievable by them. The early booking discount for airfares is a good example of this principle. Most consumers today accept the fact that different people will pay different prices for the same quality of coach-class seat on a particular flight. One explanation for why this is an accepted practice is that airfares tend to increase in price as the time of departure approaches. Thus customers who buy late and pay the higher price realize that they could have gotten a lower price if they had made their travel plans further in advance. Another example of an "achievable by me" price discount is product rebates, which are commonly used in the consumer electronics industry. Firms offering product rebates typically know that only a fraction of the buyers will follow through and take the time to send in the rebate request. By offering the rebate, however, the firm is able to advertise a lower price (selling price minus the rebate) and induce additional demand from some of the lower willingness-to-pay consumers. In this example, customers who do not follow through by sending in the rebate form still feel that they had the opportunity to get the lower price, even though they ended up paying the full price.

Compare these examples to a retailer or restaurant that offers an unannounced sale, that is, a sale price that is not widely advertised and requires the customer to specifically request it. These type of sales are common in tourist destinations, as some restaurants have special "local resident" menus that have much lower prices but must be specifically asked for. Imagine how your opinion about a restaurant would change if you were a frequent patron that just found out about this policy after paying the higher prices for years.

In summary, consumer responses to a price, or changes in the price, are based on more than just the utility theory discussed in chapter 1. Indeed, there are a number of behavioral factors that also play a role, such as reference prices, prospect theory, and the perceived fairness. Thus firms considering how to set a price, or a price change, should also factor in how customer satisfaction will be impacted by the price change. A change in customer satisfaction depends on the following:

- How the price is presented and packaged
- Perceived fairness in terms of the seller's profit
- Perceived fairness in terms of past and future prices
- Perceived fairness relative to what other customers get

# Chapter Summary

A purely analytical approach to price optimization is rarely successful because consumers do not always react in the "rational" way that traditional microeconomics predicts. Thus it is just as important to understand the psychological aspects of pricing so that price changes and promotions can be framed in a way that maximizes the probability of customer acceptance. Some of the psychological aspects of pricing that have been proven through behavioral research include the following:

- Reference pricing
- Prospect theory—the asymmetric and nonlinear treatment of gains and losses
- Perceptions of fairness (interpersonal comparisons, entitlement, and achievability)

Reference pricing refers to how consumers form a "reference price" for a particular product or service. The reference price can be set based on the consumer's experience with the prices set by other firms for similar products or services (market effect) or by the price set over a certain amount of time for your firm's product or service (time effect). One key implication of this science to pricing analytics is that firms must be careful not to offer promotion prices for too long of a period, less the consumers will form a new reference price for the product.

Prospect theory applies to pricing analytics through the finding that consumers respond unfavorably to price increases in a disproportionate manner than they respond favorably to price discounts. Thus it is typically better to frame price changes as discounts whenever possible. There is also a diminishing return to price discounts, such that a small discount may provide a favorable response that is more than twice the favorable response that a price discount of twice the dollar amount may provide.

Finally, consumers' happiness about a purchase may change based on their perceived fairness of the offer. If they feel that the company is making abnormal profits at their expense, they are less likely to be satisfied with a purchase even though their utility from owning the product is more than the purchase price they paid. Their perceptions may even change over time, especially if they find out that other consumers were able to purchase the product at a lower price and that they were excluded somehow from this offer. Thus it is generally better to design promotions such that they can be achieved by everyone, even if some consumer segments will self-select not to meet the requirements for the lower price.

# APPENDIX A

# Dichotomous Logistic Regression

Throughout this book we referred extensively to the logistic regression methodology as a means to either calibrate the logit price-response functions of chapter 1 and chapter 2 or estimate the logit bid-response probability functions introduced in chapter 4. While the two contexts exhibit many similarities in terms of their final outcome (e.g., both functions are inverse S-shaped and approach zero at some high prices), from a methodological standpoint, they require two distinct sets of statistical tools. First, the logit price-response functions are computed using non-linear regression models that attempt to minimize the sum of squared errors between the observed demand and the demand expected to materialize at the observed price points. This method, termed *nonlinear least square estimation*, requires a numeric response variable (e.g., demand) and at least one explanatory variable (e.g., price) that are assumed to be associated through a nonlinear relationship. The second method is used to estimate the logit bid-response probability functions using generalized linear regression models that maximize the likelihood of the sample data. In this case, the maximum likelihood estimation requires a dichotomous response variable (e.g., won/lost bids) and one or more numeric and/or categorical explanatory variables (e.g., price or quantity requested). We term the second method *dichotomous logistic regression*. Since the first method builds on the well-established class of linear regression models, we devote this appendix to explore some of the intricacies associated with dichotomous logistic regression models. For a comprehensive discussion of nonlinear regression models, including the logistic model, we refer the reader to Bates and Watts and Fox.[1]

## The Dichotomous Logistic Regression Model

In the general case, the dichotomous logistic model (for details, see Neter et al.) is of the form

$$Y = E\{Y\} + \varepsilon,$$

where

$$E\{Y\} = \rho(X_k) = \frac{\exp\left(\alpha + \sum_k \beta_k \cdot X_k\right)}{1 + \exp\left(\alpha + \sum_k \beta_k \cdot X_k\right)}.$$

In this expression, the variable $Y$, which takes on the values 0 and 1, is a Bernoulli random variable. $E\{Y\}$ is the expected value of $Y$; $\varepsilon$ is an error term with a distribution dependent on the Bernoulli distribution of Y; $\rho(X_k)$ is, by construction, the probability of an event happening, that is, the probability that the response variable $Y$ takes on the value 1; $X_k$ are the explanatory variables; $\alpha$ and $\beta_k$ are parameters that must be estimated by fitting the model to some historical data; and $k = 1, \ldots, K$ refers to the variables that specify the model.[2] The response function $\rho(X_k)$ is not linear in parameters $\alpha$ and $\beta_k$. If we return to the example of chapter 4 and consider that the price quoted, $P$, is the only predictor variable that explains the outcome of Alpha Company's bids, the dichotomous logistic model reduces to

$$Y = E\{Y\} + \varepsilon,$$

$$E\{Y\} = \rho(P) = \frac{\exp(\alpha + \beta \cdot P)}{1 + \exp(\alpha + \beta \cdot P)},$$

where $Y$, coded as 1 for a win and 0 for a loss, refers to the outcome of the bid, $\rho(P)$ provides the probability of winning the bid at a current price $P$, and $\alpha$ and $\beta$ are parameters that are to be computed using the historical win/loss data available.

# Linear and Logistic Regression Models for Dichotomous Response Variables

The formulation of dichotomous logistic models in terms of probabilities $p(X_k)$ provides support for why these models are typically preferred over the more simple linear regression models of the form $E\{Y\} = \alpha + \sum_k \beta_k \cdot X_k$. In particular, since the response variable $Y$ involves two event states that negate/exclude each other—in practice, a bid is either won or lost—it appears appropriate to predict the closeness of an event to these extreme 0/1 states through the means of 0/1-bounded probabilities. In this context, probabilities $p(X_k)$ close to 1 or 0 refer to events that are likely to happen (e.g., a bid is won) or not happen (e.g., a bid is lost), respectively. In contrast, the use of linear models to compute the likely state of 0/1 events typically leads to predicted values that are outside of the admissible 0/1 range such as probabilities less than 0 or greater than 1. This is particularly true when probabilities are predicted at the extreme values of the range of $X_k$'s. Since predicted values below 0 or above 1 cannot be meaningfully justified, the use of linear regression models for these situations is typically deemed inappropriate. We illustrate this problem in Figure A.1 where we employ some of the historical win/loss data from the Alpha Company and show the geometric elements recommended by comparable specifications of the linear and logistic regression models. Both models rely only on price to explain the 0/1 outcome of the bidding process. Panel A of Figure A.1 shows that if Alpha decided to quote a bid at the price of \$7, the linear model on the dichotomous 0/1 bid outcome would predict a probability close to 1.2, which carries no palpable meaning. In contrast, panel B shows that at the same bid price of \$7, the logistic regression model predicts a win probability close to 0.97.

Another reason logistic regression may be preferred over simpler linear regression when the dependent variable is dichotomous relates to how the latter violates critical assumptions of the linear models. In particular, linear models of the form $E\{Y\} = \alpha + \sum_k \beta_k \cdot X_k$ require $E\{Y\}$ to exhibit constant variance across the entire range of the $X_k$'s. This is certainly not the case when $Y$ is a Bernoulli random variable. We illustrate this point in Figure A.2, in which panel A replicates the geometric elements shown in panel A of Figure A.1 but limits prices to the price range [\$7.80,\$12.16]

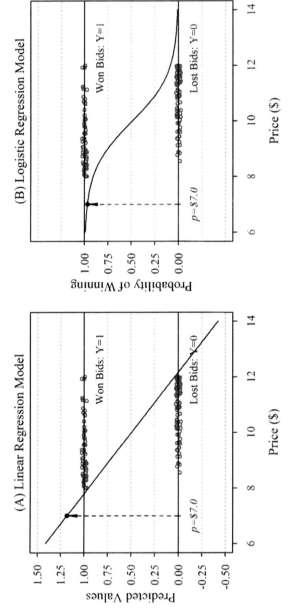

*Figure A.1. (A) Fitted line for the linear regression model, (B) fitted curve for the logistic regression model.*

within which the corresponding predicted values are bounded by 0 and 1. Within this price interval, the predicted values, $E\{Y\}$, provide information on the likelihood of Alpha winning the bids. Thus $E\{Y\}$ serves as the probability of winning the bid. A quoted price of $9.98, for example, appears to lead to a win probability of 0.50. At this price, the variance of a Bernoulli variable with parameter $p = 0.50$ is $p \cdot (1 - p)$, or 0.25. Using similar judgment, we compute the implied variance of all Bernoulli variables and chart it against the price in panel B of Figure A.2. This plot is

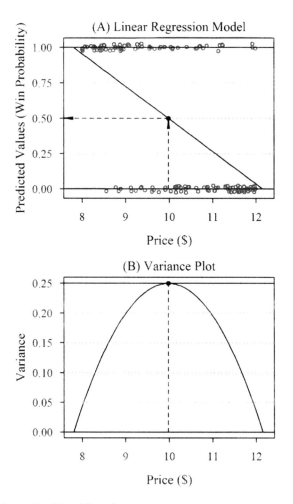

*Figure A.2. (A) Fitted line for the linear regression model, (B) variance plot.*

not linear, peaks at $9.98, and decreases symmetrically toward 0 as the price slides toward $7.80 and $12.16, respectively.

Lastly, the linear regression model is not used with dichotomous response variables because the robustness of the significance testing of parameters $\alpha$ and $\beta_k$ largely depends on the assumption that the residuals $(Y - E\{Y\})$ are normally distributed. Since $Y$ only takes on the values 0 and 1, this assumption is hard to justify, even approximately. Thus all tests of the parameter estimates $\alpha$ and $\beta_k$ computed on dichotomous responses using linear regression are questionable. Using the sample data from the Alpha Company, we show a representative residual plot in Figure A.3. In this plot, the residuals, charted against the fitted values $E\{Y\}$, are anything but normally distributed.

## The Estimation of Dichotomous Logistic Regression Models

One of the most popular techniques of estimating a logistic regression model involves the maximization of the likelihood of the observed data. For a data sample of size $n$ with a response variable $Y = \{Y_i = 0/1\}_{i = 1,n}$, the likelihood function can be expressed as

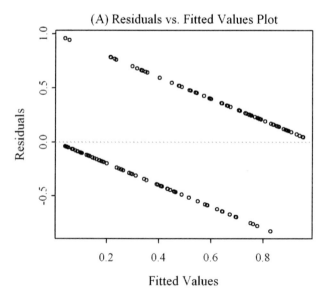

Figure A.3. Residual plot.

$$L = \prod_{i=1}^{n} \left( P_i\left(\alpha, \beta_k, X_k\right)^{Y_i} \cdot \left(1 - P_i\left(\alpha, \beta_k, X_k\right)\right)^{1-Y_i} \right),$$

where $Y_i$ is the observed 0/1 outcome for the $i$th observation, $\alpha$ and $\beta_k$ are the parameter estimates that need to be computed, $X_k$ refers to the $k$th explanatory variable, and $P_i(\alpha, \beta_k, X_k)$ is the probability $\rho_i(X_k)$ computed for the $i$th observation at the current values of $\alpha$ and $\beta_k$. Since the product form of the likelihood function leads to numerical instabilities even for small sample sizes, in practice it is generally preferred to maximize the log-likelihood function that yields the same parameter estimates but is numerically more stable. Taking the natural logarithm on both sides of the likelihood function results in the following expression for the log-likelihood function:

$$LL = \log(L) = \sum_{i=1}^{n} \left( Y_i \cdot \log\left(P_i\left(\alpha, \beta_k, X_k\right)\right) + \left(1 - Y_i\right) \cdot \log\left(1 - P_i\left(\alpha, \beta_k, X_k\right)\right) \right).$$

The maximum likelihood estimators of $\alpha$ and $\beta_k$ are obtained by evaluating the gradient of the log-likelihood function at the current values of the parameters and iteratively improving them using the information in the gradient.[3] The iterative process stops when the gradient is sufficiently close to zero. Due to the complexities involved, the iterative procedure requires the use of a general-purpose optimizer to complete the task.

Other techniques used to estimate logistic regression models rely on pure iterative methods to compute the parameters $\alpha$ and $\beta_k$. At each iteration the coefficients computed in the previous step are revised until corrections sufficiently close to zero are recommended. The Newton-Raphson method is a representative example of the iterative techniques commonly used in practice.

For the example depicted in panel B of Figure A.1, the maximum likelihood estimates are given in Table A.1. The price, with its highly statistically significant parameter $\beta$ (*p value* of 0.00), appears to indeed impact the outcome of the bid process. The negative sign of $\beta$ suggests that increases in the price quoted are to be expected to lower Alpha's probability of winning the bid. In addition, the probability plot in Figure A.1 shows that the middle part of the probability range $\rho(P)$ is almost linear in the price. This indicates that a change in the price quoted leads to approximately the same change in the probability of winning the bid,

Table A.1. Dichotomous Logistic Regression Model

|  | Estimate | Standard errors | t value | p value |
|---|---|---|---|---|
| Intercept $\alpha$ | 11.58 | 1.98 | 5.86 | 0.00 |
| Price $\beta$ | −1.16 | 0.20 | −5.96 | 0.00 |

Null deviance: 193.05 on 139 degrees of freedom
Residual deviance: 142.46 on 138 degrees of freedom
AIC: 146.46
Built-in function: glm (R base version 2.11.1)

irrespective of the reference price at which the change happens. As $\rho(P)$ approaches 1 and 0, at the extreme values of the price quoted, the curve is no longer linear.

## The Logit Link Function and the Odds Ratio

Unlike linear regression, the logistic model formulated in terms of the probability $\rho(X_k)$ does not provide for an intuitive interpretation of the parameter estimates $\alpha$ and $\beta_k$. The logit transformation linearizes the response function $\rho(X_k)$ and helps in getting an understanding of what these coefficients mean. The transformation, which calls for the natural logarithm of the ratio between $\rho(X_k)$ and its complement $(1 - \rho(X_k))$, leads to

$$\log\left(\frac{\rho(X_k)}{1 - \rho(X_k)}\right) = \alpha + \beta_k \cdot X_k,$$

where $\tilde{\rho}(X_k) = \rho(X_k) / (1 - \rho(X_k))$, referred to as the odds, describes the relative likelihood of an event happening (e.g., the relative likelihood of winning a bid). In mathematical terms, the left-hand side of the equation is called the logit link function. The existence of such a link function places the logistic regression models among the generalized linear models.[4]

Since in many applications we are interested in quantifying the change in the odds associated with a unit change in an explanatory variable $X_j$, we can write

$$\log\left(\tilde{\rho}\left(X_j + 1, X_{k,k \neq j}\right)\right) - \log\left(\tilde{\rho}\left(X_j, X_{k,k \neq j}\right)\right) = \log\left(\frac{\tilde{\rho}\left(X_j + 1, X_{k,k \neq j}\right)}{\tilde{\rho}\left(X_j, X_{k,k \neq j}\right)}\right) = \beta_j$$

or, equivalently,

$$OR = \frac{\tilde{\rho}\left(X_j + 1, X_{k, k \neq j}\right)}{\tilde{\rho}\left(X_j, X_{k, k \neq j}\right)} = \exp\left(\beta_j\right)$$

to compute the odds ratio *OR* that corresponds to a unit change in the predictor variable $X_j$ (all other explanatory variables being held constant). The odds ratio *OR* intrinsically characterizes the logistic model in that it stays constant over the entire range of any variable $X_j$. For the price-only model summarized in Table A.1, this means that a $1 increase in the quoted price *P* results in the likelihood of the firm winning the bid drop by a factor of $1/\exp(-1.16)$, or 3.19 (irrespective of what the reference price is). In this context, the price coefficient $\beta$ can be interpreted as specifying the customer price sensitivity. A large negative coefficient leads to a more price sensitive customer. The interpretation of the price coefficient can be extrapolated to apply to all other predictor variables $X_k$ (if any are present). Since the task is context specific, we restrict our discussion to providing insights only for the price quoted *P*.

In the logit link function, $\alpha$, through the antilog transformation, describes the odds of an event happening (e.g., the odds of winning the bid) when all independent variables $X_k$ are set to 0, or

$$\tilde{\rho}(X_k = 0) = \rho(X_k | X_k = 0)/(1 - \rho(X_k | X_k = 0)) = \exp(\alpha).$$

Although for the price-only model the odds are irrelevant at a price *P* of 0, it is worth noting that $\alpha$ positions the probability function along the x-axis, that is, the price axis.[5] Thus for the same value of the $\beta$ coefficient, or, equivalently, the same customer price sensitivity, the $\alpha$ values shifts the probability function to the left or to the right along the price axis such that the resulting curves are parallel to each other in their middle sections. This becomes relevant when variables other than the price enter the specification of the logistic model and are used for segmentation purposes as their presence impacts the value of $\alpha$ but not that of $\beta$. In this case, the recommended customer segments show an identical price sensitivity that may or may not be a justifiable assumption.

# The Quality of the Fit of a Dichotomous Logistic Regression Model

To assess the relative performance of competing model specifications, some performance measure is needed. A standard statistical test employed in all model-fitting exercises asks whether a model that includes explanatory variables (i.e., the full model) fits the data significantly better than a constant-only model (i.e., the null model). Similar judgment can be employed to compare logistic regression models that are nested. In this case, the null model is replaced by a reduced model that exhibits a subset of the explanatory variables of the full model.

The test statistic used to measure the relative model performance relies on the difference between the residual deviance for the full and null (or reduced) models. Since the residual deviance is a reflection of how well the log-likelihood function of a model approaches the maximum of the observed (zero) log-likelihood function, the test statistic can be expressed as

$$d = Dev_{Null} - Dev_{Full} = 2 \cdot (0 - LL_{Null}) - 2 \cdot (0 - LL_{Full}) = -2 \cdot LL_{Null} + 2 \cdot LL_{Full},$$

where $d$ is the test statistic; $Dev_{Null}$, $Dev_{Full}$, $LL_{Null}$, and $LL_{Full}$ are the deviances and the log-likelihood functions for the null and full models, respectively; 0 is the observed log-likelihood function; and 2 is a convenience, scale-parameter. The test statistic $d$ is distributed $\chi^2$ with degrees of freedom provided by the difference in the number of parameters between the full and null models.

For the logistic regression model summarized in Table A.1, the test statistic $d$ equals 50.59 (=193.05 – 142.46) and is chi-squared distributed with one degree of freedom. With an associated $p$ value of less than 0.001, this statistic tells us that our model as a whole fits significantly better than a constant-only model.

# APPENDIX B

# Pricing Analytics Using R

In this appendix, we introduce the open source statistical software environment R and show how it can be used for pricing analytics. In the coming sections, we cover basic information aimed to help you get started with R. We will illustrate specific topics and features of R while discussing these elements using real pricing problems. We combine these disparate elements into a single, standalone pricing application in the section that concludes the appendix.

## The R Environment

In a recent article in the *New York Times*, R, as a computing environment, is portrayed as being important "to the point that it's hard to overvalue it."[1] R is credited with "becoming [the data analysts'] lingua franca partly because data mining has entered a golden age, whether being used to set ad prices, find new drugs more quickly, or fine-tune financial models."[2] R's quick acceptance has been partly attributed to its being an open source environment with its users being able to access, modify, and share the source code to better answer their specific needs. Instead of offering our own explanation about what R is or is not, we encourage the reader to visit the R official website available at http://www.r-project.org to get a complete understanding of what R entails. As a summary, the following is an excerpt from the R online documentation:

> R is a language and environment for statistical computing and graphics. . . . One of R's strengths is the ease with which well-designed publication-quality plots can be produced, including mathematical symbols and formulae where needed. Great care has been taken over the defaults for the minor design choices in graphics, but the user retains full control. R is available as Free

Software under the terms of the Free Software Foundation's GNU General Public License in source code form. It compiles and runs on a wide variety of UNIX platforms and similar systems (including FreeBSD and Linux), Windows, and Mac OS. . . . The term "environment" is intended to characterize it as a fully planned and coherent system, rather than an incremental accretion of very specific and inflexible tools, as is frequently the case with other data analysis software. R, like S, is designed around a true computer language, and it allows users to add additional functionality by defining new functions. Much of the system is itself written in the R dialect of S, which makes it easy for users to follow the algorithmic choices made. For computationally intensive tasks, C, C++, and Fortran code can be linked and called at run time. Advanced users can write C code to manipulate R objects directly. . . . R can be extended (easily) via *packages*.[3]

## How to Install R and Its Contributed Packages

In this section, we describe the process of installing R and its contributed packages on a Windows-based computer. For installing R under Unix and Unix-like platforms, we refer the reader to the *R Installation and Administration* manual available at http://www.cran.r-project.org/manuals.html.[4]

The precompiled binary distributions of the base R system and contributed packages can be found on the official website of the R Project at http://www.r-project.org. If CRAN, which stands for the Comprehensive R Archive Network, is selected under the Download, Packages section, and a preferred CRAN mirror is chosen, then your Internet browser should take you to the Download and Install R web page. If a Windows installation is sought, then the Windows hyperlink should be selected to get to where the binary files are. Since the contributed packages will be installed on request, the base subdirectory should be selected next to get the Windows XP–style installer (on February 25, 2011, R version 2.12.2 was available for download). Once acquired, the installer can be run in the normal manner, for example, by double-clicking on the R-2.12.2-win.exe file in Windows Explorer. Alternatively, R can be installed directly without saving the installer locally. During the installation, users may safely select all the defaults by simply clicking the Next button on each installation screen. When the installation completes, R can be launched by selecting it from the list of all programs available in Windows. The following is a detailed list with the steps required to install R and its contributed packages.

The R installation requires the following steps:

1. Open your favorite Internet browser and go to http://www.r-project .org.
2. Under the Download, Packages section on the left-hand side of your computer screen, click on CRAN.
3. Select one of the available CRAN Mirrors (e.g., under USA, click on http://cran.cnr.berkeley.edu for the CRAN mirror from the University of California, Berkeley).
4. Under Download and Install R, click on Windows to get the precompiled binary distribution for Windows.
5. Under Subdirectories, click on base to get the binaries for the base distribution.
6. Click on Download R 2.12.2 for Windows and save the Windows installer locally in a directory of your choice (at the time of writing this book, R 2.12.2 was the last R release).
7. Open your Windows Explorer, go to the directory you chose and double-click on the Windows installer.
8. Follow the instructions to complete the R installation (for a regular user, the default options will work just fine).
9. Once the installation completes, R should appear in the list of Windows-available applications (Start/All Programs/R/R 2.12.2).

The R-contributed packages installation requires you to follow the following steps:

1. Start R (Start/All Programs/R/R 2.12.2).
2. Select Packages from the drop-down menus at the top of the R console.
3. Select Install Package(s) . . .
4. Select one of the available CRAN mirrors (e.g., USA (CA1)).

5. From the available Packages, select the ones that you would like to install (e.g., car).

6. In R type `library("Package")` to load package `Package` in the current working environment (e.g., `library("car")`).

# Getting Started With R

When you launch R in Windows, the R console opens up at which time the R environment is ready to take and execute your R commands. If you use R interactively, you are expected to type in the R commands at the command prompt. The default R prompt is >. Alternatively, you can write your commands in script or external R files that you can later run or load in the current working space using appropriate R commands (e.g., `source`). We illustrate both ways of interacting with R.

Let's suppose that you sell a product for which you have paid a unit price of $2.70. Based on prior market research, you have determined that demand $d(p)$ for this product varies linearly with the retail price $p$. The underlying product price-response function is $d(p) = 5.37 - 4.3 \cdot p$. Your intention is to compute the revenue and profit that you will likely experience at a unit retail price $p$ of $7 and $8, respectively. In R, you can calculate these elements easily as in the following R code chunk, where > is the command prompt; # introduces a comment; <- is the assignment operator; `c()` is a function that combines its attributes into a vector; +, -, and * are binary arithmetic operators; `round()` is a function that rounds the values of its first argument to (in this case) one decimal place; and `print()` is a function that prints its argument.

```
> # INPUT PARAMETERS
> D <- 53.70                        # demand intercept d(p=0)
> m <- -4.30                        # demand slope
> p <- c(7.00, 8.00)                # retail prices
> c <- 2.70                         # product cost
> # COMPUTE REVENUE
> r <- round((D + m * p) * p, 1)
> print(r)
[1] 165.2 154.4
> # COMPUTE PROFIT
> pr <- round((D + m * p) * (p-c), 1)
> pr
[1] 101.5 102.3
>
```

In R, the commands entered interactively at the command prompt are echoed automatically in the R console. One exception is the assignment operation, which is silent. In the previous example, we start by setting up four vectors to hold the elements of the price-response function (i.e., D and m), the anticipated retail prices (i.e., p), and the purchase price (i.e., c). Using the binary arithmetic operators +, -, and *, we compute in a single pass the requested entities and assign them to the appropriate vectors r and pr. All vector operations implied by +, -, and * are performed element by element with shorter vectors being recycled as needed. To show the content of the revenue and profit vectors, we use either the print() function or the direct call to the corresponding R object, in which case the call to the print() function is implicit. The first element of a vector is labeled [1], even when, as with D, m, and c, for example, we deal with one element vectors. The final R command prompt indicates that R is ready to take on, interpret, and execute another R command.

For an exploratory working session such as the previous one, working with R interactively usually suffices. However, there are many instances in practice when such an approach is not appropriate, let alone convenient. Often, if a task is envisioned to be repetitive, a series of R commands is saved in R script files that can later be loaded in an R working space on request. For example, let's suppose that we have saved a cleaned version of the previous commands in the plain text script file Revenue&Profit.R. This file may look like the following:

```
# INPUT PARAMETERS
D <- 53.70; m <- -4.30; p <- c(7.00, 8.00); c <- 2.70
# COMPUTE REVENUE
r <- round((D + m * p) * p, 1)
# COMPUTE PROFIT
pr <- round((D + m * p) * (p-c), 1),
```

where, to conserve space, we have preferred to specify the input parameters in the same line and separate them by semicolons (i.e., ;). This file can be loaded in an R session using the source command as in the R code chunk shown later in this section. As you can see, the results are identical to those of the interactive exercise we have gone through previously. In addition, you may have noticed the presence of two other convenience functions not practiced before. The rm function, called in this way, removes all objects from the current R working space. The construct involving the `setwd` function is used to set the working directory to where our script file resides (please note the use of the Unix-like path separator / even in a Windows-style working environment).

```
> # CLEAR THE WORKING SPACE
> rm(list=ls(all=TRUE))
> # SET WORKING DIRECTORY
> setwd("C:/BEP/Appendix-B")
> # LOAD SCRIPT IN THE WORKING SPACE
> source("Revenue&Profit.R")
> r
[1] 165.2 154.4
> pr
[1] 101.5 102.3
```

This section has been intended to whet your appetite for experimenting with R. As we are aware that our brief introduction and the few examples provided may be insufficient for you to get a clear understanding of what R can do for you, we refer you again to the R manuals available online at http://www.cran.r-project.org/manuals.html. Among these, *An Introduction to R* is a must lecture for those interested in becoming proficient in R.[5]

## Getting Help in R

For most R functions, documentation is provided online. To open up the documentation pages for a topic `topic`, type at the R command prompt `?topic` or `help(topic)` (e.g., `?print` or `help(c)`). At times, to get the expected behavior, you may have to surround the topic by quotation marks. For example, to get help on what `?` does, you have to type in `?"?"` or else R behaves (correctly) contrary to your expectations. If you would like to browse the documentation by yourself or just get additional resources, type `help.start()` to initialize the HTML version of the help (both offline and online behaviors are supported). To get help on the R syntax and operators, use `?Syntax` (operator syntax and precedence), `?Arithmetic` (arithmetic operators), `?Logic` (logical operators), `?Comparison` (relational operators), `?Extract` (object operators), and `?Control` (control-flow constructs).

At times, you may not know the name of your `topic` precisely. However, you could use `??topic` or `help.search("topic")` to search the help system for documentation that matches `topic` in some elements of the documentation files (e.g., name, title, alias). For example, if you forgot how to fit and handle linear models in R, you could use `help.search("linear models")` to get a multiple-entry list with all (package, function) pairs that are somehow related to your topic of choice. To review any one of the entries in the result list you could use `?package::function` (e.g., `?stats::lm`) to do so.

Many documentation pages end with executable examples. To run these examples, you have to highlight the blocks that interest you, copy them in the clipboard, and then paste them in a running instance of R. If you would like to run all examples associated with a given topic at once, you could use the `example` function to do so. For instance, `example("smooth", package = "stats")` runs all examples provided in the Example section of the `smooth` function in the `stats` package. Occasionally, you may want to load data sets available in some R contributed packages in your R working space. To list a package's available data sets or to load some or all of them in R, you could use the `data` function. For example, `data(package="rpart")` lists the four data sets available in package `rpart`. Alternatively, `data("solder", package="rpart")` loads the dataset `solder` in the running instance of R.

If you are like many of us, at times, you will find that no matter how much effort you put into solving a problem in R, you just cannot do it. Often, R, as a computing environment, may overwhelm you. Other times, the problem itself may not let you sleep at night. Whatever the reasons for your anxiety could be, do not lose faith—if you are facing a difficult problem, there is a high likelihood that someone else has faced it and solved it already. Thus we recommend that you become familiar with the features of the R forum available online at http://r.789695.n4.nabble .com. If your search of the topics already discussed, and likely solved, by the members of the R community does not lead to a successful closure, you could become a registered member and post your question(s) online. From our experience, the likelihood of not getting a timely and relevant answer from the R users is quite low.

## Common Objects in R

R operates on named objects. The most important objects in R are the vectors defined as collections of items of the same type. Currently, R supports six types of vectors: character, complex, integer, logical, numeric, and raw (for details, see ?vectors). We illustrate how vectors are set up in the next R code chunk. Vector v1 consists of five integers combined with function c(). Vector v2 is a sequence of integers that starts at 1 and goes up to 5 in increments of 1. Through simple (element by element) arithmetic operations, vectors v1 and v2 are combined to lead to vector v3. Vector v4 is a numeric sequence that runs from 1 to 2 in increments of 0.25. Vector v5 is a four-element character vector. Vector v6 evaluates to true where vector v1 is greater or equal to 15, and to false otherwise. Lastly, vector v7 is set up by repeating true, false, and NA (or missing value) two times, three times, and one time, respectively.

```
> v1 <- c(1, 15, 10, 40, 25)              # integer vector
> v1
[1] 1 15 10 40 25
> v2 <- 1:5                               # integer vector
> v2
[1] 1 2 3 4 5
> v3 <- v1^2 + 2 * v2                     # integer vector
> v3
[1]   3 229 106 1608 635
> v4 <- seq(1,2,0.25)                     # numeric vector
> v4
[1] 1.00 1.25 1.50 1.75 2.00
> v5 <- c("This", "is", "an", "example")  # character vector
> v5
[1] "This" "is"   "an"   "example"
> v6 <- (v1 >= 15)                        # logical vector
> v6
[1] FALSE TRUE FALSE TRUE TRUE
> v7 <- rep(c(TRUE, FALSE, NA), times=c(2,3,1))
# logical vector
> v7
[1] TRUE TRUE FALSE FALSE FALSE  NA
```

Often, R users have to work with subsets of the elements of vectors. These can be selected by appending to the name of the vector an index vector of the form [Index Vector]. The following illustrates the most common subsetting operations:

```
> v1[1]        # Selects 1st element of v1
[1] 1
> v1[-1]       # Selects all but 1st element of v1
[1] 15 10 40 25
> v1[1:3]      # Selects first three elements of v1
[1] 1 15 10
> v1[c(1,3,5)] # Selects first, third and fifth element of v1
[1] 1 10 25
```

```
> v1[v1 >= 25]    # Selects all elements of v1 greater or equal to 25
[1] 40 25
> v5[-c(2,3)]     # Selects all but second and third elements of v5
[1] "This"  "example"
> v7[!is.na(v7)] # Selects all non-missing values of v7
[1] TRUE TRUE FALSE FALSE FALSE
```

In addition to vectors, R operates on other types of objects as well. Matrices and arrays, multidimensional representations of vectors, are typically used with constructs that consist of elements of the same data type (e.g., numeric or character). Factors are used in connection with categorical variables that show a finite number of levels. Lists are collections of elements of different data types including lists. Data frames are special forms of lists that consist of variables of the same size and unique row names. Finally, functions are objects, too.

A technology and entertainment products retailer, such as Best Buy, who sells products in several countries across the world, could store its product prices in a matrix to facilitate the quick withdrawal of vital operations information. In the limited example provided here, subsetting the price matrix appropriately helps the retailer get the price at which Toshiba DVD players are sold in Mexico. To create the price matrix, we use the `matrix` command and force a nine-element price vector into a three-by-three data structure whose elements are filled by row. We change the column and row names of the matrix for convenience only.

```
> # ORIGINAL PRICE VECTOR IN THE LOCAL CURRENCY: USD, CAD, MXN
> p <- c(39.99, 38.49, 465, 34.99, 33.49, 405, 39.99, 38.49, 465)
> # CREATE PRICE MATRIX pm
> pm <- matrix(p, nrow=3, ncol=3, byrow=TRUE)
> colnames(pm) <- c("US (USD)", "Canada (CAD)", "Mexico (MXN)")
> rownames(pm) <- c("Philips DVD", "Toshiba DVD", "Sony DVD")
> pm
              US (USD)   Canada (CAD)   Mexico (MXN)
Philips DVD     39.99       38.49           465
Toshiba DVD     34.99       33.49           405
Sony DVD        39.99       38.49           465
> # GET THE PRICE AT WHICH TOSHIBA DVD PLAYERS ARE SOLD IN MEXICO
> pm[2,3]
[1] 405
```

In the likely event that the retailer would like to have the price information displayed by manufacturer, this can be accomplished easily by devising a three-dimension array. We illustrate this case in the following

R code chunk where we force the original nine-element price vector into a one-by-three-by-three array.

```
> # CREATE THE PRICE ARRAY BY BRAND
> pm.b <- array(p, dim = c(1, 3, 3),
    dimnames=list(c("Price"), c("US (USD)", "Canada (CAD)",
    "Mexico (MXN)"), c("Philips DVD", "Toshiba DVD", "Sony
    DVD")))
> pm.b
, , Philips DVD
          US (USD)    Canada (CAD)    Mexico (MXN)
Price      39.99         38.49            465


, , Toshiba DVD
          US (USD)    Canada (CAD)    Mexico (MXN)
Price      34.99         33.49            405


, , Sony DVD
          US (USD)    Canada (CAD)    Mexico (MXN)
Price      39.99         38.49            465
```

Often, retailers place the products they sell in distinct price tiers based on the product-perceived quality. In the previous example, the retailer groups items into two price tiers. The low-price tier consists of items priced below 37.50USD, or, equivalently, 36.20CAD and 435.20MXN, respectively. To operationalize this price classification, we create a character vector using the ifelse command that we coerce then into a factor. For both objects we use the str command to display the internal object structure.

```
> # CREATE A PRICE TIER CHARACTER VECTOR
> ptf <- ifelse(p <= c(37.5, 36.2, 435.2),
    "Low-Tier", "High-Tier")
> # SHOW INTERNAL STRUCTURE
> str(ptf)
 chr [1:9] "High-Tier" "High-Tier" "High-Tier" . . .
> # CREATE THE PRICE TIER FACTOR
> ptf <- factor(ptf)
> # SHOW INTERNAL STRUCTURE
> str(ptf)
 Factor w/ 2 levels "High-Tier","Low-Tier": 1 1 1 2 2 2 1 1 1
> ptf
 [1] High-Tier High-Tier High-Tier Low-Tier Low-Tier Low-Tier
 [7] High-Tier High-Tier High-Tier
Levels: High-Tier Low-Tier
```

In certain cases incentives exist for organizations to store several data elements in the same data constructs. The retailer we introduced in the previous examples may find it beneficial to keep the list of countries it serves, the list of brands it sells, and the prices it charges in the same data object. As these data elements are of different types (i.e., character and numeric objects), we group them together in a list using the `list` command. We then illustrate how various elements of the list can be queried for easy information withdrawal or data reuse.

```
> # CREATE THE LIST
> country <- c("US", "Canada", "Mexico")
> brand <- c("Philips", "Toshiba", "Sony")
> ls <- list(Country = country, Brand = brand, Price = pm)
> ls
$Country
[1] "US"     "Canada" "Mexico"

$Brand
[1] "Philips" "Toshiba" "Sony"

$Price
                US (USD)    Canada (CAD)    Mexico (MXN)
   Philips DVD    39.99         38.49           465
   Toshiba DVD    34.99         33.49           405
   Sony DVD       39.99         38.49           465

> # DISPLAY BRAND LIST
> ls$Brand
[1] "Philips" "Toshiba" "Sony"
> # SHOW THE PRICE AT WHICH TOSHIBA DVDs SELL IN MEXICO
> ls$Price[2,3]
[1] 405
```

We conclude this section by referring to the data object that you will experience the most if you intend to become proficient in R. To this end, data frames are special lists used for storing data tables. Unlike matrices, data frames do not have to consist of data elements of the same type. We illustrate this subtle point by creating a data frame that bundles the numeric price vector with the price tier factor and the character country vector and displays them together in a table-like format. We create the data frame using the `data.frame` command. We show the first four rows (or the header) using the `head` command. Finally, we display the internal structure of the object using the `str` command.

```
> # CREATE THE DATA FRAME
> df <- data.frame(Price = p, Tier = ptf,
+ Country = rep(country, 3), stringsAsFactors=FALSE)
> # SHOW HEADER (WITH 4 ENTRIES)
```

```
> head(df, n = 4)
      Price     Tier            Country
  1   39.99     High-Tier       US
  2   38.49     High-Tier       Canada
  3   465.00    High-Tier       Mexico
  4   34.99     Low-Tier        US
> # SHOW INTERNAL OBJECT STRUCTURE
> str(df)
'data.frame':  9 obs. of 3 variables:
 $ Price  : num 40 38.5 465 35 33.5 ...
 $ Tier   : Factor w/ 2 levels "High-Tier","Low-Tier": 1 1 1 2 2 2 1 1 1
 $ Country: chr "US" "Canada" "Mexico" "US" ...
```

# Writing Functions in R

Since functions are R objects, we could have discussed them in the previous section. However, due to their importance in executing repetitive tasks, we prefer to discuss them at length in this section.

R functions are defined using the reserved word `function`, which is followed by a possibly empty list of formal arguments. These arguments are provided to the function in round brackets. The argument list is followed by the body of the function supplied in curly brackets. When the function is called, the formal parameters supplied by the user (if any are present) are used to evaluate the R expressions provided in the function's body. The general syntax for defining a function is

```
fun.name <- function(arg1[=def1], arg2[=def2], ...) {R expressions},
```

where `def1` and `def2` are optional default values for formal arguments `arg1` and `arg2`. The function is called by using `fun.name(arg1= val1, arg2= val2, . . .)`, where `val1` and `val2` could take on the default values `def1` and `def2` or some other user-specified values. To facilitate the (re)use of the results returned by the function, the function call is usually assigned to a data element as the following:

```
result <- fun.name(arg1= val1, arg2= val2, ...)
```

The `result` data element consists of all elements that the function returns through an explicit call to the `return` statement. Alternatively, if `return` is missing, the function returns the value of the last evaluated expression from the body of the function.

We illustrate the practical use of writing R functions with one of the examples discussed in chapter 2. The juvenile products retailer computed for one of its representative products a linear price-response function with an intercept *a* of 53.7 and a slope *b* of –4.3. Given the cost of $2.50 incurred by the retailer to acquire the good, we intend to write a simple R function to help the product manager compute the optimal retail price for this product. We build the `opt.price` function such that the characteristics of the price-response function, the cost incurred, and an optimization control parameter are the function's only formal arguments. For convenience, we associate these arguments with some default values, which tend to follow the figures the retailer experienced with this item. The optimization control parameter refers to a starting value for the optimization search algorithm—we consider that a value of $5 is a reasonable default value for this parameter. With these arguments, we construct the price-dependent profit function that we intend to maximize. Keeping things at a generic level, we express the profit function as the product between the quantity expected to materialize at a price point $p$ (i.e., $a + b \cdot p$) and the unit profit associated with that price point (i.e., $p - cost$). We then call the built-in R function `optim` to solve for the optimal price. For internal argument compliance, we supply `optim` with values for all its required and some of its optional arguments. In addition to the parameters that we already discussed, we make use of `fnscale` to specify that we intend to maximize the profit function and `method` to indicate our optimization method preference. Finally, we ask the function to return the result of the price optimization step.

```
opt.price <- function(a=53.7, b=-4.3, cost=2.5, st.val=5.0) {
   # DEFINE THE PROFIT FUNCTION
   profit.function <- function(p, a=a, b=b, cost=cost)
                      {(a + b*p)*(p-cost)}
   # MAXIMIZE THE PROFIT FUNCTION
   res <- optim(par=st.val, fn=profit.function, a=a, b=b,
      cost=cost, method=c("BFGS"), control=list(fnscale=-1))
   # RETURN OBJECT res
   return(res)
} # end opt.price
```

To compute the product optimal price, the product manager can call `opt.price` in many equivalent ways. Since we provided argument defaults that are specific to this problem, the following function calls can all be used interchangeably:

```
opt.price()                                          # call 1
opt.price(53.7, -4.3, 2.5, 5.0)                      # call 2
opt.price(a=53.7, b=-4.3, cost=2.5, st.val=5.0)      # call 3
opt.price(st.val=5.0, cost=2.5, b=-4.3, a=53.7)      # call 4
opt.price(st.val=5, cost=2.5)                        # call 5
```

In the first call, since no user-defined arguments are supplied, the function uses the default values to pass to the R expressions present in the body of the function. In the second call, since no names for arguments are provided, R matches these by their position. In the third call, arguments are fully specified by their names and values. Here, the argument matching is done by name—a named argument is matched to the formal argument that carries the same name. Name matching takes precedence over positional matching. This is illustrated in the fourth call, where even though the position of the arguments has changed, the R environment is capable of correctly matching all arguments provided. Last but not least, the fifth call shows that after the name matching takes place, R relies on the default values for the remaining of the arguments to complete the task. Any of these five equivalent function calls recommends an optimal product retail price of $7.49 as the following depicts:

```
> opt.price(a=53.7, b=-4.3, cost=2.5, st.val=5)
$par
[1] 7.49
$value
[1] 107.25
$counts
function gradient
       7        3
$convergence
[1] 0
$message
NULL
```

As we mentioned in one of the previous paragraphs, functions are suited for repetitive tasks. Imagine that the product manager reviews the latest trends in the product sales and updates the parameters of the price-response function to 65.5 and −5.6 for $a$ and $b$, respectively. If nothing else changes, the updated optimal price of $7.10 can be easily computed with a function call of the following form:

```
> opt.price(a=65.5, b=-5.6, cost=2.5, st.val=5)
$par
```

```
[1] 7.10
$value
[1] 118.40
$counts
function gradient
    7         3
$convergence
[1] 0
$message
NULL
```

Moreover, if the product manager were in charge of the pricing function for hundreds or thousands of products, a function to compute individual optimal prices based on minimum input arguments would come in handy.

We conclude this section by referring readers interested in deepening their understanding of how to write efficient functions in R to chapter 10 of the R manual *An Introduction to R*, available at http://www.cran.r-project.org/manuals.html.

## Handling External Files in R

R as a statistical computing environment can load data from database management systems (DBMSs) such as Oracle and Teradata or external data files. Since a discussion on how R interacts with the growing number of DBMSs is beyond the scope of this book, we focus on how R handles external data files.

Often, the external data files that R needs to deal with are plain text files. Typically, these files consist of data entries that are delimited either by white space or by special characters or at preset locations on each input line. Among the character-delimited text files, tab-delimited and comma-separated values files are commonly used in many industry applications. The fixed width text files impose a maximum width for each of the fields in the file and are easier to inspect visually but require more storage space. We illustrate how R handles both of these types of files using the read.table and read.fwf commands.

Returning to the example of the juvenile products retailer, let's suppose that the characteristics of the price-response functions have been computed for all products. A limited subset of this information is depicted in comma-delimited and fixed-width formats. Note the presence of the pipe character | in the header of the fixed width file—while this character is not needed in different working environments, we use such a construct here to make sure that the data-loading step completes successfully in R.

```
##### Comma Separated Values File #####
############# Product.csv #############
Product,Cost[$],Intercept,Slope
V4C3D5R2,2.5,53.7,-4.3
V4C3D5R3,3.0,47.9,-3.9
V4C3D5R4,2.3,59.8,-4.5
########## Fixed Width File ##########
############# Product.txt #############
Product |Cost[$]|Intercept|Slope
V4C3D5R2   2.5      53.7     -4.3
V4C3D5R3   3.0      47.9     -3.9
V4C3D5R4   2.3      59.8     -4.5
```

Assuming that the two plain text files are saved in the working directory `C:\BEP\Appendix-B`, we can read them in R using the commands provided in the next code snippet. We use `read.table` and `read.fwf` to load the comma-separated values file and the fixed-width file, respectively. For a successful data load, we provide relevant input values for some of the functions' formal arguments. In both cases, we acknowledge the presence of a header at the top of the file (`header`), we impose the classes to be assumed by the various data fields (`colClasses`), and we intentionally do not check the syntactic validity of the variable names to account for the presence of special characters such as $ (`check.names`). For each of the commands, we provide appropriate entries for the field or the header separators (`sep`). For `read.fwf` we specify the widths in number of characters of the fixed width fields (`widths`). Last but not least, we check with `str` that the files loaded correctly and inspect the first entry in each file with `head`.

```
> # SET WORKING DIRECTORY
> setwd("C:/BEP/Appendix-B")
>
> # READ COMMA DELIMITED FILE
> data1 <- read.table("Product.csv", header=TRUE, sep=",",
+ colClasses=c("character", rep("numeric", 3)), check.
  names=FALSE)
> str(data1)
'data.frame': 3 obs. of 4 variables:
$ Product : chr "V4C3D5R2" "V4C3D5R3" "V4C3D5R4"
$ Cost[$] : num 2.5 3 2.3
$ Intercept: num 53.7 47.9 59.8
$ Slope : num -4.3 -3.9 -4.5
> head(data1,1)
```

```
      Product Cost[$] Intercept Slope
1 V4C3D5R2    2.5    53.7 -4.3
>
> # READ FIXED WIDTH FILE
> data2 <- read.fwf("Product.txt", widths=c(9,8,10,5),
   header=TRUE,
+ sep="|", colClasses=c("character", rep("numeric", 3)),
+ check.names=FALSE)
> str(data2)
'data.frame':  3 obs. of 4 variables:
 $ Product : chr "V4C3D5R2 " "V4C3D5R3 " "V4C3D5R4 "
 $ Cost[$] : num 2.5 3 2.3
 $ Intercept: num 53.7 47.9 59.8
 $ Slope   : num -4.3 -3.9 -4.5
> head(data2,1)
   Product Cost[$] Intercept Slope
1 V4C3D5R2    2.5    53.7 -4.3
```

Up to this point, we assumed that the external files were known explicitly. In many cases, however, the external data files have to be selected from long lists of candidate files. For example, imagine that a plain-text file similar in content to Product.csv file is generated for all product categories that the retailer sells. Furthermore, imagine that these files share the same location with other thousands of files that are important yet irrelevant for the tasks the product manager needs to take care of. In instances like this, R can be of help if the category level files are named consistently based on well-defined naming patterns. If this is the case, R can search a specified directory for files whose names match a prespecified regular expression. The product manager can then work only with those files that satisfy the search requirements.

To provide an illustrative example, we consider that the category-level files at the juvenile products retailer are saved following the name convention CT_DTS_NP.csv, where CT is a 12-character unique category identifier, DTS is a 14-character date and time stamp, and NP is an up to three-character auxiliary element that provides the number of items in the category CT. To identify all files that qualify from the current directory, we use the list.files command with the appropriate input value for its pattern argument. Specifically, we construct a regular expression that follows the built-in name convention and relies on certain classes of characters to attempt the match. In this context, [[:alnum:]]{12}, for example, refers to a string that consists of exactly 12 alphanumeric characters. In contrast, [[:digit:]]{1,3} refers to a string that consists of one, two, or three numerical digits. Altogether, three files with their names displayed in the following code chunk qualify for further investigation. The savvy reader should check and make sure that the identified files do indeed follow the preset name convention.

```
> # SET WORKING DIRECTORY
> setwd("C:/BEP/Appendix-B")
> # GET THE FILES THAT MATCH THE PATTERN
> files <- list.files(path=".",
+ pattern = "^[[:alnum:]]{12}_[[:digit:]]{14}_[[:digit:]]
  {1,3}.csv")
> files
[1] "T12389XLT654_20110412141535_879.csv"
[2] "V12345SLT987_20110412141529_234.csv"
[3] "X14879ABC962_20110412141540_63.csv"
```

We conclude this section with a few thoughts on how R interacts with data files native to other computing environments such as SAS, Stata, and SPSS. The `foreign` package included with the R base distribution provides several functions that facilitate the import of such files in R. Among these, `read.xport`, `read.dta`, and `read.spss` allow R to operate on data files native to SAS, Stata, and SPSS, respectively. For more details on this topic, we encourage you to consult the *R Data Import/Export* manual available at http://www.cran.r-project.org/manuals.html.[6]

# Running R Scripts

In one of the introductory sections of this appendix, we briefly referred to R scripts and how they can be loaded and executed in a running instance of R with the `source` command. Since R scripts deserve a little more attention, we return to this topic to focus on other points of interest.

To begin with, Windows-based R has its own script editor that can be launched by selecting `New Script` under the `File` drop-down menu. While writing R scripts, commands for editing and executing them are available in both `File` and `Edit` menus of the R GUI interface. However, since the R user interface targets primarily R power users, writing scripts in R may turn out to be an intimidating task for novice R users. If this is your case, we recommend you write your scripts in a familiar text editor (e.g., Notepad++, WinEdt), save them with the .R extension, and either copy/paste or `source` them in R. We also recommend you to show patience and perseverance toward working in R—your effort is profitable and will pay off shortly.

Often, in a production environment you would like to run R scripts in a noninteractive way—that is, without launching R explicitly and manually executing your scripts within the running instance of R. If you were a retailer, for example, you might have to post-process all your daily sales data from hundreds of stores every night at midnight. You would do this to get the most recent sales trends in all sales areas that you serve or to explore the current performance of a newly introduced product. In this case, instead of opening your R environment (likely remotely) and instructing R to run your scripts, you would rather schedule your working environment to run the scripts without supervision at precisely 12:00 a.m. No matter what your reason is to have R run noninteractively, you can do it easily under Windows or any other operating system that supports the installation of R. For Windows users, providing that the path to the R executable is part of the `path` environment variable, R can be called to run noninteractively from the Windows command prompt with a construct such as the following:

```
R CMD BATCH --no-restore --no-save Revenue&Profit.R Revenue&Profit.Rout,
```

where `R CMD BATCH` instructs R to run noninteractively your R script `Revenue&Profit.R`, `--no-restore` instructs R not to load any saved R workspace if one exists in the current directory, `--no-save` instructs R that no data sets are to be saved at the end of the R session, and `Revenue&Profit.Rout` is the name of the file to which the output is written. To improve your efficiency further, you can include this command in a batch file and ask the Windows scheduler to execute this file at 12:00 a.m. every night. A setup like this helps you focus more on what your business needs are and less on technical details that are not always error-free. For more details on these topics, we encourage you to consult the *An Introduction to R* manual available at http://www.cran.r-project .org/manuals.html.

## Pricing Analytics Using R

In this section we build on skills and knowledge we acquired previously and use R to solve a complete pricing problem. In doing so, we recycle some of the R code we already discussed. We provide details relevant to our problem next.

Often, organizations need to decide on how much they should charge their customers for the products or services requested. At times, they should also investigate whether or not the pricing strategies currently in place still align with the evolving market requirements. Since in many instances the two concepts overlap significantly, in what follows, we focus on the former task of determining the optimal product/service prices. In our example, we assume that the organization—the juvenile products retailer—did some market research and computed the price-response functions for all its products. We further assume that these functions, together with the cost information, are available locally (vs. remotely) in comma-delimited files organized by product category (see the following for a relevant snapshot of the file content). As it is quite likely that they are the outcome of an automated process, these files follow the naming convention discussed in a previous section of this appendix.

```
######### PRODUCT CATEGORY INPUT FILE ##########
###### X14879ABC962_20110412141540_63.csv ######
Product,Cost[$],Intercept,Slope
A4F5X9F2,4.8,89.4,-4.5
A4F5X9F3,4.6,90.3,-4.3
A4F5X9F4,4.9,85.7,-4.8
(removed 60 more entries)
```

Our goal is to write efficient R code to help us compute the optimal product prices based on the available inputs. We show the final version of our R script in the code snippet that follows this paragraph. After we clear the working space and set the working directory, we identify the files that qualify for the task based on name pattern matching. We keep our code generic as the product breadth and depth do not impact our approach. We then load the files sequentially in R and combine their content in a master product data frame. We use by, an R construct that applies a function to a data frame split by a factor, to compute the optimal prices for all products and product categories. We format the output and merge it to the original data. We show a snapshot of the results in Table B.1, where the first column is shown for convenience only and is not part of the R output. We supplement these business insights with intelligence on the shape of the product profit functions, an example of which we depict in Figure B.1. Due to space restrictions, we do not provide the R code that creates these figures; it builds, however, on the `plot` command and its many fine-tuning formal arguments. Our R script being kept generic offers you, our savvy reader, at least one important benefit. Specifically, if you were to replicate our results, all you have to change in our code would be the path to the working directory where the input files reside. This is an add-on benefit that comes with good (R) programming habits.

```
### CLEAR THE WORKING SPACE
rm(list=ls(all=TRUE))
### SET WORKING DIRECTORY
setwd("C:/BEP/Appendix-B")

### FUNCTION TO COMPUTE THE OPTIMAL PRICE
opt.price <- function(x) {
  # INITIALIZE INPUT PARAMETERS
  a<- x[1,3]; b<-x[1,4]; cost<-x[1,2]; st.val=5
  # DEFINE THE FUNCTION TO BE MAXIMIZED
  obj.fun.linear <- function(p, a=a, b=b, cost=cost)
    {(a + b*p)*(p—cost)}
  # MAXIMIZE THE FUNCTION
  res <- optim(par=st.val, fn=obj.fun.linear, a=a, b=b,
    cost=cost, method=c("BFGS"), control=list(fnscale=-1))
  # RETURN OBJECT res
  return(res)
} # end opt.price

### READ AND COMBINE THE CATEGORY DATA FILES
files <- list.files(path=".",
  pattern="^[[:alnum:]]{12}_[[:digit:]]{14}_[[:digit:]]
    {1,3}.csv")
for (findex in 1:length(files)) {
  data.tmp <- read.table(file=files[findex], header=TRUE,
    sep=",",
    colClasses=c("character", rep("numeric", 3)),
    check.names=FALSE)
  if (findex == 1) {data <- data.tmp}
    else {data <- rbind(data, data.tmp)}
} # end for findex
### COMPUTE THE OPTIMAL PRICES FOR ALL PRODUCTS
res <- by(data, factor(data[,1]), FUN=opt.price,
  simplify=TRUE)
res <- do.call("rbind", res)
# FORMAT OUTPUT
res <- data.frame(res[,1:2], Product=row.names(res))
res <- res[,c(3,1:2)]
names(res) <- c("Product", "Optimal Price", "Expected
  Profit")
res[,2] <- unlist(res[,2])
res[,3] <- unlist(res[,3])
### MERGE RESULTS
data <- merge(data, res)
```

*Table B.1. Product-Level Optimal Prices and Expected Profits*

| Product category | Product | Cost ($) | Intercept | Slope | Optimal price ($) | Expected profit ($) |
|---|---|---|---|---|---|---|
| X14879ABC962 | A4F5X9F2 | 4.8 | 89.4 | −4.5 | 12.3 | 255 |
| X14879ABC962 | A4F5X9F3 | 4.6 | 90.3 | −4.3 | 12.8 | 289 |
| X14879ABC962 | A4F5X9F4 | 4.9 | 85.7 | −4.8 | 11.4 | 201 |
| ... | | | | | | |
| T12389XLT654 | V4C3D5R2 | 2.5 | 53.7 | −4.3 | 7.5 | 107 |
| T12389XLT654 | V4C3D5R3 | 3.0 | 47.9 | −2.9 | 9.8 | 132 |
| T12389XLT654 | V4C3D5R4 | 2.3 | 59.8 | −3.5 | 9.7 | 191 |
| ... | | | | | | |
| V12345SLT987 | Z4F3D5T6 | 7.2 | 115.9 | −2.3 | 28.8 | 1073 |
| V12345SLT987 | Z4F3D5T7 | 6.0 | 130.8 | −2.8 | 26.4 | 1160 |
| V12345SLT987 | Z4F3D5T8 | 6.5 | 120.3 | −2.5 | 27.3 | 1083 |
| ... | | | | | | |

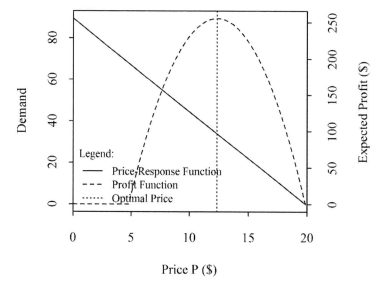

*Figure B.1. Price-response function, profit function, and the optimal price (product: A4F5X9F2).*

# Notes

## Chapter 1

1. Brownell et al. (2009).
2. Ayers (2003).
3. Ayers (2003).
4. Goodwin et al. (2004).
5. Espey and Espey (2004).
6. Dalhuisen et al. (2003).
7. Fogarty (2005), chap. 2.
8. Gallet and List (2003).
9. Goodwin et al. (2004).
10. Fogarty (2005), chap. 2.
11. Fogarty (2005), chap. 2.
12. Espey and Espey (2004).
13. Tellis (1988).

## Chapter 2

1. Cudahy and Coleman (2007).
2. Simon (1989), p. 30.
3. R Development Core Team (2011a); SAS Institute Inc. (2011); StataCorp (2009).
4. Little (1970); Lilien et al. (2007); Simon (1989); Wuebker et al. (2008).
5. Consulting and software companies such as CoreMatrix LLC and Tealeaf Technology Inc. provide their customers with such specialized services.
6. Gaur and Fisher (2005).
7. See the concept of decision calculus in Little (1970); Wuebker et al. (2008), pp. 51–54.
8. Wuebker et al. (2008), pp. 54–68.
9. Simon (1989), p. 36; Wuebker et al. (2008), p. 68.
10. See, for example, Greene (2003).
11. See, for example, Greene (2003).
12. Achabal, McIntyre, and Smith (1990); Cooper, Baron, Levy, Swisher, and Gogos (1999); Foekens et al. (1994); Foekens et al. (1999); Narasimhan (1984); Smith and Achabal (1998).

13. Cooper et al. (1999); Trusov et al. (2006).
14. Narasimhan (1984).
15. Achabal et al. (1990); Foekens et al. (1994, 1999); Narasimhan (1984).
16. Narasimhan (1984); Smith and Achabal (1998).
17. Cooper et al. (1999).
18. Foekens et al. (1994).

# Chapter 3

1. See, for example, Elmaghraby and Keskinocak (2003).
2. See, for example, Gallego and Van Ryzin (1994); Talluri and Van Ryzin (2004).
3. InterContinental Hotels Group (2009); Carlson Hotels Worldwide (2009).
4. Bichler et al. (2002); Narahari et al. (2005).
5. Fisher and Raman (2010), p. 31.
6. Lazear (1986); Pashigan (1988); Pashigan and Bowen (1991).
7. Fisher (2009).
8. Jacobs (2008).
9. Pashigan (1988); Pashigan and Bowen (1991).
10. Polonski and Morgan-Vandome (2009).
11. AMR Research (n.d.).
12. Walker (1999).
13. Wolfe (1968).

# Chapter 4

1. Details on successful customized pricing implementations in industries such as package delivery, building products distribution, and hotel event space are provided in Kniple (2006); Dudziak (2006); Hormby and Morrison (2008); and Hormby et al. (2010), respectively.
2. Phillips (2005b); Kadet (2008).
3. Boyd et al. (2005).
4. Logit model: Boyd et al. (2005); Phillips (2005a); Agrawal and Ferguson (2007); Ferguson (2010). Power model: Agrawal and Ferguson (2007).
5. Garrow et al. (2006).
6. Phillips (2005a).
7. Boyd et al. (2005); Phillips (2005a); Agrawal and Ferguson (2007).
8. Phillips (2005a).
9. Kadet (2008).
10. Wedel and Kamakura (1998).
11. Hosmer and Lemeshow (2000); Kutner et al. (2004).

# Chapter 5

1. Kahneman and Tversky (1979).
2. Kahneman et al. (1986).

# Appendix A

1. Bates and Watts (1988); Fox (2002).
2. Neter et al. (1999).
3. In this context, the gradient refers to the vector of partial derivatives of the log-likelihood function taken with respect to $\alpha$ and $\beta k$. Finding the parameter estimates that make the gradient zero is equivalent to maximizing the log-likelihood function.
4. Nelder and Wedderburn (1972); Fox (2008).
5. For the price-only model summarized in Table A., the odds of winning the bid at a price $P$ of \$0.0 equal exp(11.58), or 106,937.5.

# Appendix B

1. Vance (2009).
2. Vance (2009).
3. R Development Core Team (2011a).
4. R Development Core Team (2011b).
5. Venables et al. (2011).
6. R Development Core Team (2011c).

# References

Achabal, D. D., McIntyre, S., & Smith, S. A. (1990). Maximizing profits from periodic department store promotions. *Journal of Retailing, 66*(4), 383–407.

Agrawal, V., & Ferguson, M. E. (2007). Bid-response models for customized pricing. *Journal of Revenue and Pricing Management, 6*(3), 212–228.

AMR Research. (2008). *Lifecycle price management—Winning in a down economy*. Presentation at the 6th Annual Retail Technology Summit, Berlin, Germany, October 15–16.

Ayers, C. (2003). *Microeconomics*. Upper Saddle River, NJ: Pearson.

Bates, D. M., & Watts, D. G. (1988). *Nonlinear regression analysis and its applications*. New York, NY: John Wiley & Sons.

Bichler, M., Lawrence, R. D., Kalagnanam, J., Lee, H. S., Katircioglu, K., Lin, G. Y., . . . Lu, Y. (2002). Applications of flexible pricing in business-to-business electronic commerce. *IBM Systems Journal, 41*(2), 287–302.

Boyd, D., Gordon, M., Anderson, J., Tai, C., Yang, F., Kolamala, A., . . . Haas, S. (2005). Manugistics. Target pricing system. *Patent No: US 6963854 B1*. Washington, DC: U.S. Patent and Trademark Office.

Brownell, K. D., Farley, T., Willett, W. C., Popkin, B. M., Chaloupka, F. J., Thompson, J. W., & Ludwig, D. S. (2009). The public health and economic benefits of taxing sugar-sweetened beverages. *New England Journal of Medicine, 361*(16), 1599–1605.

Carlson Hotels Worldwide. (2009). Carlson Hotels breaks the property system paradigm (press release). Retrieved July 1, 2011, from http://www.hospitality upgrade.com/_magazine/magazine_Detail.asp?ID=375

Cooper, L. G., Baron, P., Levy, W., Swisher, M., & Gogos, P. (1999). PromoCast: A new forecasting method for promotion planning. *Marketing Science, 18*(3), 301–316.

Cudahy, G., & Coleman, G. L. (2007). The price is right . . . Isn't it? *Outlook, 2*. Retrieved January 20, 2011, from http://www.accenture.com/us-en/outlook/Pages/outlook-journal-2007-pricing-strategies.aspx

Dalhuisen, J. M., Florax, R. J. G. M., de Groot, H. L. F., & Nijkamp, P. (2003). Price and income elasticities of residential water demand: A meta-analysis. *Land Economics, 79*(2), 292–308.

Dudziak, B. (2006). Senior manager in the planning and analysis group at BlueLinx. Panelist in Non-Traditional Industries Workshop. Georgia Institute of Technology and Revenue Analytics 2nd Annual Conference on Price Optimization and Revenue Management, Atlanta, GA, May 18, 2006.

Elmaghraby, W., & Keskinocak, P. (2003). Dynamic pricing in the presence of inventory consideration: Research overview, current practices, and future directions. *Management Science, 49*(10), 1287–1309.

Espey, J. A., & Espey, M. (2004). Turning on the lights: A meta-analysis of residential electricity demand elasticities. *Journal of Agricultural and Applied Economics, 36*(1), 65–81.

Ferguson, M. E. (2010). Customized price response to bid opportunities in competitive markets. In J. J. Cochran, L. A. Cox, P. Keskinocak, J. P. Kharoufeh, & J. C. Smith (Eds.), *Wiley encyclopedia of operations research and management science* (p. 9). New York, NY: John Wiley & Sons.

Fisher, M. (2009). Rocket science retailing: The 2006 Philip McCord Morse lecture. *Operations Research, 57*(3), 527–540.

Fisher, M., & Raman, A. (2010). *The new science of retailing: How analytics are transforming the supply chain and improving performance.* Boston, MA: Harvard Business School Press.

Foekens, E. W., Leeflang, P. S. H., & Wittink, D. R. (1994). A comparison and exploration of the forecasting accuracy of a loglinear model at different levels of aggregation. *International Journal of Forecasting, 10*(2), 245–261.

Foekens, E. W., Leeflang, P. S. H., & Wittink, D. R. (1999). Varying parameter models to accommodate dynamic promotion effects. *Journal of Econometrics, 89*, 249–268.

Fogarty, J. (2005). *Wine investment, pricing and substitutes* (Doctoral dissertation). University of Western Australia, Crawley, Western Australia.

Fox, J. (2002). *An R and S-PLUS companion to applied regression.* Thousand Oaks, CA: Sage Publications.

Fox, J. (2008). *Applied regression analysis and generalized linear models* (2nd ed.). Thousand Oaks, CA: Sage Publications.

Gallego, G., & Van Ryzin, G. J. (1994). Optimal dynamic pricing of inventories with stochastic demand over finite horizons. *Management Science, 40*(8), 999–1020.

Gallet, C. A., & List, J. A. (2003). Cigarette demand: A meta-analysis of elasticities. *Health Economics, 12*(10), 821–835.

Garrow, L., Ferguson, M. E., Keskinocak, P., & Swann, J. (2006). Expert opinions: Current pricing and revenue management practices across U.S. industries. *Journal of Revenue and Pricing Management, 5*(3), 248–250.

Gaur, V., & Fisher, M. L. (2005). In-store experiments to determine the impact of price on sales. *Production and Operations Management, 14*(4), 377–387.

Goodwin, P., Dargay, J., & Hanly, M. (2004). Elasticities of road traffic and fuel consumption with respect to price and income: A review. *Transport Reviews, 24*(3), 275–292.

Greene, W. (2003). *Econometric analysis.* Englewood Cliffs, NJ: Prentice Hall.

Hormby, S., & Morrison, J. (2008). *Is bigger really better? Bulk pricing and negotiated deals.* Instructors for workshop, Marriott International, Georgia Institute of Technology and Revenue Analytics 4th Annual Conference on Price Optimization and Revenue Management, Atlanta, GA. November 11, 2008.

Hormby, S., Morrison, J., Dave, P., Meyers, M., & Tenca, T. (2010). Marriott International increases revenue by implementing a group pricing optimizer. *Interfaces, 40*(1), 47–57.

Hosmer, D., & Lemeshow, S. (2000). *Applied logistics regression* (2nd ed.). New York, NY: Wiley Series in Probability & Statistics.

InterContinental Hotels Group. (2009). IHG launches price optimization module (press release). Retrieved July 1, 2011, from http://www.revenueanalytics .com/pdf/601_IHG_Press_Release.pdf

Jacobs, K. (2008, May 29). *Sears Holdings posts unexpected loss on markdowns.* Retrieved April 1, 2011, from http://www.reuters.com

Kadet, A. (2008). Price profiling. *Smart Money, 17*(5), 81–85.

Kahneman, D., Knetsch, J. L., & Thaler, R. (1986). Fairness as a constraint on profit seeking: Entitlements in the market. *American Economic Review, 76*(4), 728–741.

Kahneman, D., & Tversky, A. (1979). Prospect theory: An analysis of decision under risk. *Econometrica, 47*(2), 263–292.

Kniple, J. (2006). Director of pricing strategy and solutions at UPS. Panelist in Non-Traditional Industries Workshop. Georgia Institute of Technology and Revenue Analytics 2nd Annual Conference on Price Optimization and Revenue Management. Atlanta, GA, May 18, 2006.

Kutner, M., Nachtsheim, C., & Neter, J. (2004). *Applied linear regression models* (4th ed.). Boston, MA: McGraw-Hill.

Lazear, E. P. (1986). Retail pricing and clearance sales. *American Economic Review, 76*, 14–32.

Lilien, G. L., Rangaswamy, A., & De Bruin, A. (2007). *Principles of marketing engineering* (1st ed.). Bloomington, IN: Trafford Publishing.

Little, J. D. C. (1970). Models and managers: The concept of a decision calculus. *Management Science, 16*(8), 466–485.

Narahari, Y., Raju, C. V. L., Ravikumar, K., & Shah, S. (2005). Dynamic pricing models for electronic business. *Sadhana, 30*(2–3), 231–256.

Narasimhan, C. (1984). A price discrimination theory of coupons. *Marketing Science, 3*(2), 128–147.

Nelder, J. A., & Wedderburn, R. W. M. (1972). Generalized linear models. *Journal of the Royal Statistical Society. Series A, 135*(3), 370–384.

Neter, J., Kutner, M. H., Nachtsheim, C. J., & Wasserman, W. (1999). *Applied linear statistical models* (4th ed.). Chicago, IL: Irwin/McGraw-Hill.

Pashigan, B. P. (1988). Demand uncertainty and sales: A study of fashion and markdown pricing. *American Economic Review, 78*(5), 936–953.

Pashigan, B. P., & Bowen, B. (1991). Why are products sold on sale? Explanation of pricing regularities. *Quarterly Journal of Economics, 106*(4), 1015–1038.

Phillips, R. L. (2005a). *Pricing and revenue optimization.* Stanford, CA: Stanford Business Books.

Phillips, R. L. (2005b). *Pricing optimization in consumer credit.* Presentation at the 2005 INFORMS Annual Meeting, San Francisco, CA.

Polonski, J., & Morgan-Vandome, A. (2009). *Oracle retail solution: Retail application footprint.* Presentation at the North American Retail Partner Summit, January 28.

R Development Core Team. (2011a). *R: A language and environment for statistical computing.* Vienna, Austria: R Foundation for Statistical Computing. Retrieved from http://www.R-project.org

R Development Core Team. (2011b). *R Installation and administration.* Vienna, Austria: R Foundation for Statistical Computing. Retrieved from http://cran.r-project.org/doc/manuals/R-admin.pdf

R Development Core Team. (2011c). *R data import/export.* Vienna, Austria: R Foundation for Statistical Computing. Retrieved from http://cran.r-project.org/doc/manuals/R-data.pdf

SAS Institute Inc. (2011). *SAS software.* Cary, NC: SAS Institute. Retrieved from http://www.sas.com

StataCorp. (2009). *Stata statistical software.* College Station, TX: StataCorp LP. Retrieved from http://www.stata.com

Simon, H. (1989). *Price management.* New York, NY: North Holland.

Smith, S. A., & Achabal, D. D. (1998). Clearance pricing and inventory policies for retail chains. *Management Science, 44*(3), 285–300.

Talluri, K. T., & Van Ryzin, G. J. (2004). *The theory and practice of revenue management.* Boston, MA: Kluwer Academic.

Tellis, G. J. (1988). The price elasticity of selective demand: A meta-analysis of econometric models of sales. *Journal of Marketing Research, 25,* 331–341.

Trusov, M., Bodapati, A. V., & Cooper, L. G. (2006). Retailer promotion planning: Improving forecast accuracy and interpretability. *Journal of Interactive Marketing, 20*(3–4), 71–81.

Vance, A. (2009, January 6). Data analysts captivated by R's power. *New York Times.* Retrieved April 1, 2011, from http://www.nytimes.com

Venables, W. N., Smith, D. M., & R Development Core Team. (2011). *An introduction to R.* Vienna, Austria: R Foundation for Statistical Computing. Retrieved from http://cran.r-project.org/doc/manuals/R-intro.pdf

Walker, J. (1999). A model for determining price markdowns of seasonal merchandise. *Journal of Product and Brand Management, 8*(4), 352–361.

Wedel, M., & Kamakura, W. (1998). *Market segmentation: Conceptual and methodological foundations.* International Series in Quantitative Marketing. Norwell, MA: Kluwer Academic.

Wolfe, H. B. (1968). A model for control of style merchandise. *Industrial Management Review, 9*(2), 69–82.

Wuebker, G., Baumgarten, J., Schmidt-Gallas, D., & Koderisch, M. (2008). *Price management in financial services: Smart strategies for growth.* Burlington, VA: Ashgate.

# Index

# Announcing the Business Expert Press Digital Library

*Concise E-books Business Students*
*Need for Classroom and Research*

This book can also be purchased in an e-book collection by your library as

- a one-time purchase,
- that is owned forever,
- allows for simultaneous readers,
- has no restrictions on printing,
- can be downloaded as PDFs from within the library community.

Our digital library collections are a great solution to beat the rising cost of textbooks. E-books can be loaded into their course management systems or onto students' e-book readers.

The **Business Expert Press** digital libraries are very affordable, with no obligation to buy in future years.

For more information, please visit **www.businessexpertpress.com/librarians**. To set up a trial in the United States, please contact **Sheri Dean** at sheri.dean@globalepress.com; for all other regions, contact **Nicole Lee** at nicole.lee@igroupnet.com.

---

## OTHER TITLES IN OUR MARKETING STRATEGY COLLECTION
### Collection Editor: **Naresh Malhotra**

- *Developing Winning Brand Strategies* by Lars Finskud
- *Conscious Branding* by David Funk
- *Marketing Strategy in Play: Questioning to Create Difference* by Mark Hill
- *Decision Equity: The Ultimate Metric to Connect Marketing Actions to Profits* by Piyush Kumar and Kunal Gupta
- *Building a Marketing Plan: A Complete Guide* by Ho Yin Wong, Kylie Radel, and Roshnee Ramsaran-Fowdar
- *Top Market Strategy: Applying the 80/20 Rule* by Elizabeth Rush Kruger

0  1341  1571224  9

| DATE DUE | RETURNED | [ |
|----------|----------|---|
|          |          |   |
|          |          |   |
|          |          |   |
|          |          |   |
|          |          |   |
|          |          |   |
|          |          |   |
|          |          |   |
|          |          |   |
|          |          |   |
|          |          |   |
|          |          |   |
|          |          |   |
|          |          |   |
|          |          |   |
|          |          |   |
|          |          |   |
|          |          |   |

CPSIA information can be obtained at www.ICGtesting.com
Printed in the USA
BVOW08s1103140813

328434BV00005B/19/P

9 781606 492574